simply
living well

simply
living well

A GUIDE TO CREATING A
NATURAL, LOW-WASTE HOME

Julia Watkins

Houghton Mifflin Harcourt
Boston New York 2020

www.hmhbooks.com

Library of Congress Cataloging-in-Publication Data
Names: Watkins, Julia, author.
Title: Simply living well : a guide to creating a natural, low-waste home / Julia Watkins.
Description: Boston : Houghton Mifflin Harcourt, 2020. | Includes bibliographical references and index. | Summary: "Easy recipes, DIY projects, and other ideas for living a beautiful and low-waste life, from the expert behind @simply.living.well on Instagram"-- Provided by publisher.
Identifiers: LCCN 2019045719 (print) | LCCN 2019045720 (ebook) | ISBN 9780358202189 (hardback) | ISBN 9780358192695 (ebook)
Subjects: LCSH: Home economics. | House cleaning. | Formulas, recipes, etc. | Waste minimization. | Kitchen gardens.
Classification: LCC TX158 .W37 2020 (print) | LCC TX158 (ebook) | DDC 640--dc23
LC record available at https://lccn.loc.gov/2019045719
LC ebook record available at https://lccn.loc.gov/2019045720

Book design by Ashley Lima

Line art by Kotkoa/Shutterstock (endpapers); Bodor Tivadar/Shutterstock (p. xv); Pimlena/Shutterstock (p. xvi); Allison Meierding (pp. 17, 18, 19); Kate Macate/Shutterstock (p. 66); Geraria/Shutterstock (pp. 112, 166, 208)

Printed in China

TOP 10 9 8 7 6 5 4 3 2 1

To my Granny Eloise and my Great Uncle Ben—
and their very special namesakes

CONTENTS

PROJECTS AND RECIPES

INTRODUCTION

I like to think this is a book your grandmother could have given you. Chock-full of tips, recipes, and remedies, this book is her hand held out, sharing what in her day felt ordinary but seems extraordinary today. Of course, she didn't write this book—she lived it. As for me, I had to learn it first, then live it, and only then start to write it down, all while striving for a simple, slow, sustainable life in line with the principles of zero-waste.

If you're new to zero-waste, in a nutshell it's a growing movement to reduce what you consume and throw away. There's a bit of a misconception about what zero-waste means, with stories and photos of people fitting five years of trash in a pint-size jar. What's often not shown is the long and arduous process of stumbling, experimenting, and learning that got them there. Zero-waste is a process, not an event—much more about trying for zero than being at zero. In fact, most proponents of zero-waste acknowledge that generating absolutely no waste is all but impossible. Instead, they recommend doing what makes sense for you and what you feel you can sustain, getting as close to zero as you can and following—in order—the 5Rs of zero-waste: refuse, reduce, reuse, recycle, and rot (or compost).

Now, a word about recycling. It's by far the most common approach, but also the most misleading. If you were to peek into the average American kitchen or bathroom, you'd be hard-pressed to find anything not wrapped with, bottled in, or made of plastic. What may surprise you is that only 9 percent of that plastic gets recycled, with the rest dumped in landfills, oceans, or incinerators, releasing harmful toxins into the environment. Unlike glass or metal, plastic cannot be recycled indefinitely. Instead, most plastics are downcycled a handful of times before becoming so degraded they can't be reused again. At that point, there's no choice but to throw them away. As materials go, plastic is cheap to make, easy to use, and often a real challenge to avoid. But minimizing your use of plastics, rather than relying on recycling, is one of the best ways to reduce your waste and your impact on the earth.

Fundamentally, starting your pursuit of zero-waste means looking carefully at how you consume and what kinds of waste that produces. Everyone's different, but even a cursory audit of your consumption habits ought to reveal opportunities to cut back on waste.

It also sometimes helps to put your habits in a broader context, which to me means asking whether you're part of the linear economy or the circular economy. Most of our economy is still a linear economy, where resources are extracted, processed, consumed, and discarded. Take a paper coffee cup—there's a straight line running from a tree in the forest through the paper mill, the manufacturing plant, the coffee shop, your hand, the trash can, and a landfill.

There's nothing sustainable about a linear economy. At some point, we'll either run out of trees or space in the landfill or both. And even where forests are replanted, most often we're replacing old-growth forests and all their rich biodiversity with tree plantations that at best comprise just a few species of trees.

In a circular economy, we're still extracting at least some of our resources, though with a bit more thought and a lot more care. For example, there are ways to manage certain types of resource extraction so they align more with natural cycles of regeneration. And once extracted, resources can be processed and utilized in a way that anticipates value in a product even after it has been used by a consumer, at which point it can be repurposed, reused, remanufactured, or otherwise refurbished. In a circular economy, we avoid creating waste (and minimize what little waste we do produce) by keeping things continually in use, in one form or another.

A great deal of the circular economy is accomplished by smarter designs, innovative materials, technological advances, and radically different business models. But there's a lot—and I mean *a lot*— you can do in your own home, often by looking back to a time when the demands of feeding a family of four were no different than they are today, but with no fancy supermarkets or big box stores down the road or fast and easy take-out or delivery options a phone call away.

This is why, for me, zero-waste has been about so much more than just avoiding trash or preventing waste. It's been about changing my mindset, developing an inner resourcefulness, and creating deep, meaningful connections to the natural world, my ancestors, my food, my health, and my community. The recipes and tips in this book reflect those values every bit as much as they offer ways for individuals to reduce their personal waste while demanding responsibility from businesses and governments.

My first encounter with zero-waste was in Africa, nearly twenty years ago. I was serving in the Peace Corps and living in a remote village in the West African country of Guinea. Rural, roadless, and entirely off the grid, life in my village was resolutely zero-waste—mostly because there was so very little to waste in the first place. Practically everything was made by hand, often from materials drawn directly from the natural world. Manufactured goods that did find their way to the village, once they'd fulfilled their intended function, were repurposed and reused, usually until they had nearly disintegrated from so much wear and tear. Nothing, it seemed, was ever thrown away.

Zero-waste popped up again in my life about a decade later, not long after my first child was born. I found myself dealing with a litany of health issues, and to help me get better I turned to a wide range of holistic treatments. I sought to recover my health by following many of the same slow, simple rhythms of being and of making I had witnessed in Africa or remembered from my grandmother's kitchen. So many of the ideas, recipes, and remedies in this book reflect those old ways of living as much as they involve modern nutrition and natural medicines.

Around this time, I also became exceedingly conscious of our material possessions. I'd like to say it happened because I was a naturally mindful person. But what woke me up was having to move three times in eight years, once across town and twice across the country. Nothing beats having to sort through every single item you own, wrap it in tissue, pack it into boxes, lug it onto trucks, and then haul it inside, unpack it, and organize it all over again. You can only do this so many times with something (or really, most things) before you're convinced you'll be happier without it. With each move, I got rid of nearly two-thirds of our possessions until all that was left was what we truly needed. If stuff begets stuff, the concept works just as well in reverse. Getting rid of some things made it easier to get rid of other things, so much so that living with less stuff and consuming more mindfully became a way of life. I think novelist Pico Iyer said it best: "Luxury is not a matter of all the things you have, but rather all the things you can afford to live without."

In the midst of working on my health and paring down our possessions, I also became interested in the old ways of doing things, which translated to learning a lot of new skills. I learned to cook from scratch, bake my own bread, and prepare foods in traditional ways. I made rich bone broths, butter, yogurt, and cheese. I canned fruits and veggies and fermented anything I could fit into a glass jar. I taught myself to knit and crochet, sew (a little), and clean the old-fashioned way (a lot). I cloth-diapered my babies, hung a clothesline in my backyard, planted a veggie garden, and set up a composting system. I experimented with making my own bath and body products, learned how to make remedies from herbs, adopted some basic waste-free shopping habits, and practiced shopping secondhand until it became second nature. Of course, none of this happened overnight. And not all of it stuck. Really, I just tried to follow my interests and experiment with whatever piqued my curiosity—taking little steps here and there, using what I had, doing what I could. It's remarkable how much joy can be found in making even one small simple change.

With almost everything I did, I sought out the wisdom rooted in traditional cultures and, especially, the habits and practices of my grandparents. Of course, what we call simple, natural, nontoxic, organic living, my grandparents just called life. What were everyday tasks for them were new endeavors for me. I do appreciate the comforts many of us enjoy from this past century of progress. But I'm equally aware of what we traded away for the conveniences of modern life. A lot of us will never know the practical hardships faced by those who lived a hundred years ago. But a lot of them never knew the social, emotional, and spiritual hardships that today grow only more acute as technological advances move us farther away from our food, our communities, and maybe even ourselves. I don't advocate turning your back on the world. But I do think there's no better way to enrich your life than learning about the way things used to be and weaving into your daily routine at least a few time-honored practices and traditions whose simplicity and charm nourish the mind, body, and spirit.

This isn't just about going retro, either. It's also good for the environment—the way we used to do things was far more gentle on the earth. I am astounded, and more than a little concerned, by how much plastic waste has found its way into virtually every place on the planet, from the top of Mount Everest to the depths of the Mariana Trench. Each year, around 8 million tons of plastic wind up in the ocean, and global plastic production is expected to double by 2050. Many plastics take around 450 years to break down, with microscopic plastic particles accumulating in ecosystems and across the food chain. Already, at least half the world's sea turtles and around 90 percent of the world's seabirds have been found to have ingested some form of plastic. By midcentury, the amount of plastic in the ocean is expected to outweigh the amount of fish. For me, this means the care I put into our household isn't just about finding nifty substitutes for single-use packaging and trying to get to that pint-size jar of trash at year's end. Learning some of the old ways and striving for zero-waste is how I live my values and do my part for future generations.

Of course, when it comes to the many environmental challenges facing the planet—air and water pollution, climate change, deforestation, species loss, and so on—it will take vision and leadership from governments, international organizations, and even the private sector to drive meaningful change at a global scale. I can see how tempting it is to think: "What good will it do if I cut way back on my trash when everyone else around me isn't doing a thing?" But our individual choices do matter. Maybe not in a strictly numerical sense, in terms of tons of plastic or parts per million of atmospheric carbon dioxide. But when enough people start making the same kinds of choices, markets, politicians, and even laws tend to follow along. Personally, the choices I make every day make me feel good. I draw inspiration and energy from trying to make my little part of the world a better, healthier, more beautiful, and more sustainable place.

It is my hope that this book will serve as a bridge between the can-do ethos of generations past and the earth-conscious mindfulness many of us seek to capture and bring into our lives today. It celebrates simplifying, slowing down, working with your hands, making more, buying less, valuing quality over quantity, and living frugally, self-sufficiently, and harmoniously with the natural world. It encourages wasting less and revering the ways our grandparents or, depending on your age, great-grandparents solved all manner of problems— feeding their families, cleaning their clothes, and caring for their bodies, minds, and spirits. It manifests the idea that people can live simply *and* well.

By the time you're finished reading this book, you'll know how to make your own cleaning supplies, natural remedies, and bath and body products. You'll know how to use simple ingredients, plants from your backyard, and herbs from your garden to clean a grass stain, soothe a headache, and stave off a cold. I can't promise, but I would wager that learning to make things instead of buying them will give you a new level of self-confidence and a deep and restorative sense of satisfaction. If you're anything like me, you'll find at least a glimmer of truth in that old saying *happy hands make for happy hearts*. Hope you enjoy!

LOW-WASTE
KITCHEN

When I first decided to try for zero-waste, the kitchen was my primary focus: Since so much of our household waste came from food, it seemed a good place to start. To begin, I tried to create a simple, minimalist space that would help me remember to create less waste by consuming (and discarding) less stuff. I took an inventory of our kitchen appliances, gadgets, and dishes and pared them down to the bare essentials. I found I had four whisks, so I thrifted three of them. When I noticed I had a blender, a Vitamix, and a food processor, I downsized to one. I donated my slow cooker and decided that one large soup pot would do. I gave away all but eight spoons, forks, and knives for my family of four and kept two out of five cutting boards.

To reduce waste in the kitchen, I thought a lot about my grandmother's habits around shopping and storing food, and also turned to countless ideas from the zero-waste community. Seeing my kitchen through that lens, I contemplated ways to refuse what I didn't need, reduce what I used, reuse or repurpose what I had, and repair and compost what I could. I set a goal to make recycling a last resort.

A lot of this involved simply swapping disposable products for nondisposable ones. I learned to shop with reusable bags, became well acquainted with the bulk section at the grocery store, and started using glass jars and containers for everything—rice, coffee, meat, you name it. I also taught myself ways to store and preserve food to cut back on waste. When berries started to wilt in the refrigerator, I froze them to use later in smoothies; when vegetables looked like they weren't going to be eaten immediately, I chopped them and turned them into fermented foods that could last for months. Once I had used up all the plastic-handled scrub brushes and disposable sponges I owned, I replaced them with wooden-handled brushes and cloth towels. I got rid of trash can liners and looked for ways to reuse food scraps—or compost them. Finally, when I grew tired of buying staples like hummus and ketchup in plastic containers, I taught myself how to make them from scratch. All told, my family reduced our waste enough to replace our ten-gallon trash can with a one-gallon galvanized mop bucket.

To this day, we still produce trash, and I suspect we always will. Not every food is available in bulk. Even finding apples without those little stickers on them can be a challenge. And when it comes to household items, sometimes buying things without a lot of packaging just isn't possible. I'm game for making my own apple cider vinegar, but if that little light bulb in the refrigerator burns out, I know that means a trip to the store and probably some plastic packaging that can't be recycled. Life circumstances sometimes get in the way too—I'm not too proud to admit that there are times when the demands of work and parenting make it all but impossible not to cut corners. In our convenience culture, that often means I end up buying pre-cooked meals in plastic containers or prepared snacks in single-use wrappers. I do what I can and give it my best, remembering that living sustainably has to feel sustainable. In this chapter, I hope you'll find ideas and support for reducing waste in the kitchen, while remembering to be gentle with yourself. As John Steinbeck wrote in *East of Eden*, "Now that you don't have to be perfect, you can be good."

ZERO-WASTE KITCHEN SWAPS

One of the best ways to reduce waste in the kitchen is to swap disposable items for reusable ones. But before you start tossing out all your old things, remember that zero-waste is ultimately about using fewer resources and buying less stuff. Think about how your grandparents would have solved a problem or met a need, particularly while living by the motto "use it up, wear it out, make it do, or do without." Don't be fooled into thinking that you need to buy your way to a simpler, more sustainable lifestyle. Instead, use up disposables and plastics until they no longer serve their purpose and *then* replace them with a more sustainable option. If you can find an item secondhand—terrific! If you can use a reusable item for multiple purposes—even better! A mason jar, for example, can serve as a drinking glass, water bottle, storage jar, or to-go container. Ultimately, you get to decide what you need. Here are a few ideas to help you brainstorm.

LOW-WASTE GROCERY SHOPPING

Grocery shopping presents a significant opportunity for reducing waste. There are rolls of plastic bags waiting to be used in the produce and bulk shopping aisles, and the cashier almost always insists on bagging already-packaged meat, poultry, and fish in an extra plastic bag. Many grocery stores still use plastic bags at checkout. In the United States alone, 100 billion plastic bags are produced and used each year, and only 1 percent of those bags get properly recycled. Most items in a grocery store come in some form of disposable packaging, whether it be berry cartons, yogurt cups, or plastic shampoo bottles. Everything is packaged for convenience—even vegetables can be found chopped, prewashed, and packaged in plastic bags and shrink-wrapped containers. Although you likely can't achieve zero landfill waste, with a bit of preparation, planning, and organization, you can significantly reduce your shopping footprint. Here are a few tips to support low-waste shopping:

EAT REAL FOOD. Shop the periphery of the supermarket, where you'll find fresh produce, meat, and fish, foods our grandmothers would have recognized. This is real food, and it's typically better for your health and usually far away from the packaged and processed foods stocked in the middle aisles. Focus on buying produce that is fresh, unpackaged, and, whenever possible, in season and locally sourced.

INSTEAD OF	CHOOSE
Plastic trash bags	Newspaper bin liners (see page 19) or brown paper bags
Single-use plastic shopping bags	Reusable cloth shopping bags
Single-use produce and bulk bags	Reusable cotton produce and bulk bags
Plastic bread bags	Reusable cotton bread bags (or pillowcases)
Disposable paper towels	"Unpaper towels"—reusable cloth towels or rags
Disposable napkins	Reusable cloth napkins
Microfiber cloths (contain plastic)	Cotton or hemp rags, bar mop towels
Plastic scrub brushes	Wooden, compostable scrub brushes
Disposable sponges	Biodegradable sponges, loofah pads, Swedish towels
Plastic food storage containers, disposable take-out containers	Glass or stainless steel containers, mason jars
Disposable coffee cups/mugs	Reusable coffee cups/mugs
Disposable water bottles	Water filter and reusable water bottles, mason jars
Disposable plastic straws	Stainless steel, glass, or bamboo straws
Disposable cutlery	Stainless steel or bamboo cutlery
Plastic cooking utensils	Wooden or stainless steel utensils
Plastic-packaged liquid dish soap	Package-free bar soap (castile or savon de Marseilles)
Commercial cleaning supplies	Homemade, nontoxic cleaning supplies (see page 70)
Single-use plastic wrap, single-use aluminum foil	Beeswax food wraps, cloth container covers
Single-use parchment paper	Compostable parchment paper, silicone baking mats
Plastic sandwich or storage bags	Reusable storage bags (silicone or cloth)
Plastic lunchboxes or bento boxes	Stainless steel lunch boxes
Plastic ice trays and ice pop molds	Stainless steel or silicone ice trays and ice pop molds
Single-use muffin liners	Silicone or compostable parchment muffin liners
Single-use spice containers	Reusable jars and bulk spices
Single-use tea bags	Reusable tea infuser and bulk tea
Disposable coffee pods	French press or coffee maker and reusable coffee filters
Teflon cookware	Cast-iron cookware
Plastic cutting boards	Wooden cutting boards
Disposable gloves	Compostable rubber gloves
Plastic lighter	Wooden matches

INVEST IN AND SHOP WITH CLOTH BAGS, GLASS JARS, OR OTHER REUSABLE CONTAINERS. Buy some good-quality reusable bags for produce, bread, and bulk items (or see page 9 to make your own drawstring bags). Lightweight mesh and cotton bags are ideal for shopping for fresh produce and many dried bulk foods. You'll also want a supply of glass jars, stainless containers with lids, or Tupperware for foods that can't be carried in cloth bags, such as ground coffee, meat, and salad bar items. To prevent paying extra for using your own bags and containers, be sure to let the cashier know the container's "tare" (weight when empty). To find the tare, ask the clerk at customer service to weigh the container for you before you fill it. They can either write the weight on the bottom of the container using a wax pencil or you can record the weight in a notebook or the notes section of your phone. Then this amount can be subtracted from the final weight at checkout. Although this might sound complicated, cashiers already know to do this when customers use the store's containers at the salad/soup bar or bulk aisle.

SHOP BULK BINS FOR DRIED FOODS. As much as possible, buy from the bulk bins to avoid unnecessary food packaging. Foods commonly available in bulk bins include grains, nuts, dried beans, seeds, cereals, pretzels, trail mix, dried fruits, and chocolate. If you're lucky, you may even have access to bulk items like vinegar, soy sauce, olive oil, laundry soap, shampoo, and conditioner. In my experience, stores like Whole Foods, Earth Fare, Bulk Barn, Sprouts, and local independent food co-ops usually have well-stocked bulk bins and support zero-waste shopping. Record each bulk item's price look-up (PLU) code using a wax pencil or in the notes section on your phone; this is what the cashier uses to ring up each item. If you become a regular zero-waste shopper, you'll have a running list of numbers of foods you often buy in bulk. You may even have them memorized after a few months.

BUY UNPACKAGED FRUITS AND VEGETABLES. Avoid produce packaged in single-use bags and cartons and opt instead for loose fruits and vegetables. If you run out of cloth produce bags, place produce loose in your cart. While this may not work for a pound of loose mushrooms or green beans, it's certainly possible for produce like bananas, melons, broccoli, cucumbers, lettuce, oranges, and apples. In most cases, using individual plastic bags to shop for produce is a habit more than a necessity.

BUY FRESH BAKED GOODS USING YOUR OWN BAGS. Instead of buying packaged breads and pastries, buy them fresh from the bakery using a reusable cloth bread bag. If you don't have a bread bag, a small clean pillowcase works well, too. You can either buy the bread whole or ask for it to be sliced.

BUY CHEESE FROM THE CHEESE COUNTER USING YOUR OWN CONTAINER. Avoid prepackaged cheese and instead shop at the grocery store's cheese counter. Ask to have a wedge cut off a cheese wheel and placed directly in your reusable container. You'll be given a very sticky price sticker—if you don't want to spend a lot of time washing and peeling it off the container, ask if you can carry it in your pocket and present it at checkout.

BUY OLIVES FROM THE OLIVE BAR USING YOUR OWN CONTAINER. In recent years, several chain grocery stores have installed olive bars stocked with everything from cheese-filled peppers to pickled okra, grilled artichokes, cornichons, and garlic-stuffed olives. Use your own container to shop at olive bars. Just tare your jar at customer service and then fill it up. There's no need to write a PLU number, as most stores use a single PLU for foods bought at salad, hot, or olive bars.

BUY COFFEE FRESH FROM THE COFFEE BINS USING YOUR OWN BAG OR GLASS JAR. If your grocery store has a coffee counter, you can skip buying coffee in plastic or paper bags. You can buy whole beans or, if you prefer ground coffee, there's often a coffee grinder onsite. In my experience, there isn't a scale at the coffee counter, so you'll need to tare your coffee jar at customer service ahead of time. I recommend using a glass jar, but a reusable cotton bag works fine too—you'll just need to wash it afterward.

BUY MEAT USING YOUR OWN CONTAINER (IF YOUR STORE WILL ALLOW IT). Since there's always a scale at the meat counter, the butcher can easily tare your container before placing fish, chicken, or poultry in it. As with cheese, if you don't want the price sticker placed on your container (they're very hard to remove), ask the butcher to hand it to you so you can present it to the cashier at checkout.

IF BUYING PACKAGED FOOD, AVOID PLASTIC AND OPT FOR RECYCLABLE MATERIALS. If you must buy packaged foods, buy products packaged in recyclable materials. Recycling paper, glass, and metal is a complete cycle, while plastic generally is not. The stark reality is that more than 90 percent of plastic goes straight to a landfill. The best one can hope for with the remaining 10 percent is that it gets downcycled—turned into low-quality material such as doormats, textiles, and plastic lumber. After one round of being downcycled, these products usually end up in a landfill.

BUY UNPACKAGED SOAP. Check the bath and body section of your grocery store to see if they sell bulk and/or unpackaged soap. Some stores even sell liquid soap, shampoo, and conditioner in bulk. Bring your own tared glass jar for the liquid soaps and a reusable cloth bag for bar soap.

BUY ECO-FRIENDLY HOUSEHOLD GOODS. Buy toilet paper packaged in paper rather than plastic. If you can't find it locally, consider buying it online and in bulk. Ditch paper towels and invest in reusable cloths instead. Buy parchment paper, sandwich bags, and muffin cups made from compostable paper, such as the kind sold by brands like If You Care. Switch out plastic wrap and aluminum foil for beeswax wrap and reusable glass containers. Unless you make your own dish or laundry detergent (see pages 91 and 98), consider buying detergents packaged in cardboard boxes rather than plastic. If you do buy plastic, buy the largest size.

REFUSE A RECEIPT OR REQUEST A PAPERLESS COPY. Refuse receipts by either asking that one not be printed or having it emailed to you, if possible.

CREATE A ZERO-WASTE SHOPPING KIT. Keep a shopping kit in your car or on a hook by the door. Include items such as reusable shopping, produce, bulk, and bread bags, as well as glass jars, stainless steel storage containers, a reusable coffee mug, a reusable water bottle, cloth napkins, reusable cutlery, and a stainless steel straw.

SHOP AT STORES THAT SUPPORT ZERO-WASTE. In addition to zero-waste grocery stores popping up around the country, small, local, independent stores and cooperatives are often more flexible and willing to support shopping "out of the box" by letting customers use their own containers. Farmers' markets and CSAs are good options as well. And by shopping locally and seasonally, we also reduce invisible forms of waste, such as the energy spent on production, processing, and transportation. Not everyone has access to stores that offer foods and goods in bulk; if you do, do your best to support them. The website www.litterless.com has a list by state of stores that allow you to purchase staples in your own containers.

BUILD RELATIONSHIPS WITH GROCERS, FARMERS, AND CLERKS. Author Michael Pollan calls this shaking the hand that feeds you. Whether you're shopping at grocery stores or farmers' markets, zero-waste food shopping presents a great opportunity to build relationships with grocers, farmers, and store clerks in your community. Depending on where you live, you could be the norm or the outlier when it comes to your specific shopping routine and style. If you are an outlier, you may have to explain why you want to use your own container for cheese and pastries. If you can keep the tone light and friendly, you might be surprised at how willing people are to help you get what you want. As my mother-in-law says, diplomacy is the fine art of letting others get your way.

REUSABLE DRAWSTRING BAGS

One of the easiest ways to reduce disposable waste in the kitchen is to replace plastic shopping bags with reusable ones. You can either buy cloth bags or—if you have beginner sewing skills—you can make them yourself. I make these simple drawstring bags for purchasing dried goods in bulk. While muslin is an ideal material, you can also repurpose old, lightweight pillowcases or sheets if you have them.

Most bags sold today have a label with the tare (empty weight—see page 4) sewn conveniently into the seam. If you make your own bags, I suggest taking them to the customer service desk at your grocery store and asking them to weigh them for you. You can either write the tare on the bag with a permanent marker or record it in the notes section of your phone. If they're all made from the same fabric and are about the same size, you'll just need to remember one tare, which will make checkout swift and easy.

MATERIALS

Cotton muslin fabric	*Sewing machine*
Iron	*Thread*
Measuring tape	*5 feet of cord*
Scissors	*Safety pin*

DIRECTIONS

1. Wash, dry, and iron the fabric.

2. For a large bag, cut an 11-by-29-inch rectangle. For a medium-size bag, cut a 9-by-25-inch rectangle.

3. Mark ½ inch from the top and bottom (short) ends of the fabric. Fold the fabric along these marks, iron it in place, and sew. These will be hems.

continued

4. Mark 1 inch from both hemmed short ends, fold the fabric over, iron it in place, and sew. These will be the casings for the drawstring.

5. Fold the fabric in half, bringing the short edges together, with the right sides facing and the hems facing out. Press along the fold.

6. Stitch all the way around the bag, leaving a ½-inch seam allowance. Be sure to start and stop below the top casing you created for the drawstring.

7. Turn the bag right side out.

8. Cut two pieces of cord, each double the width of your bag plus 8 inches. The length of cord for the large bag would be 30 inches. The length of cord for the medium-size bag would be 26 inches.

9. Attach a safety pin to the end of one piece of cord. Starting on one side, thread it through both casings until it comes out the same side it started.

10. Attach a safety pin to the other piece of cord and feed it through the same casings but in the opposite direction (starting and ending on the other side).

11. Tie the loose ends of the cord on each side together. Pull on each side to cinch your bag together.

HOMEMADE BEESWAX WRAPS

Beeswax wraps hit the market a few years ago, providing a brilliant and sustainable alternative to disposable plastic wrap and aluminum foil. If you've used them, you know they're essentially a piece of beeswax-infused cloth you can shape and mold around food. They can be used to cover bowls and dishes, insulate rising bread, store halves of fruits and veggies, and wrap sandwiches. The wax coating protects food from moisture while still allowing it to breathe. As with produce bags, you can either buy them or make them yourself. See page 128 for more information on buying and working with beeswax. **Makes: 3 wraps, sizes small, medium, and large**

MATERIALS

100% cotton fabric	*Dedicated paintbrush*
Iron	*Baking sheet*
Scissors or pinking shears	*Compostable parchment paper*
Measuring tape	*Kitchen tongs*
¼ cup powdered pine resin	*Used newspapers*
¼ cup grated beeswax	*Clothespins and clothes drying rack*
4 teaspoons jojoba oil	

DIRECTIONS

1. Wash, dry, and iron the fabric. Cut out 3 squares: 8 by 8 inches, 11 by 11 inches, and 14 by 14 inches. For a neat edge, and to prevent fraying, you can use pinking shears, although it's not necessary.

2. Preheat the oven to 225°F.

3. In a bowl, combine the pine resin, beeswax, and jojoba oil.

4. Line a baking sheet with compostable parchment paper and place one fabric square on it. Sprinkle about one-third of the wax mixture evenly all over the fabric.

continued

5. Bake for 10 to 12 minutes, until the wax mixture has melted.

6. Remove the baking sheet from the oven and brush the beeswax mixture evenly over the fabric. (The beeswax will stick to the brush, so be sure to use something you don't mind reserving for future beeswax projects.)

7. Pop the baking sheet back in the oven for a couple of minutes to allow the wax to melt evenly.

8. Remove the baking sheet from the oven. Lift the fabric with kitchen tongs and allow excess beeswax to drip onto the parchment paper. With newspapers underneath to catch any drips, use clothespins to hang the beeswax wrap on the drying rack to dry and cool.

9. Repeat with the remaining fabric squares.

TO USE Use the pressure and warmth of your hands to mold the wrap around food and containers. To clean, hand-wash in cold water with mild soap. Hang over a dish rack to dry. Once the wraps are worn out, make a new set and toss the old ones in the compost heap.

REUSABLE CLOTH CONTAINER COVERS

As an alternative to aluminum foil, plastic wrap, and wax paper, cloth container covers keep consumables protected and contaminant-free. They're also an ideal way to repurpose old fabric scraps. I like to make them in different sizes—small ones make great mason jar covers, while larger ones can be used to cover bowls, pots, or crocks. If you're wondering if they're easy to clean, the answer is yes, yes, yes! If they're not too dirty, you can hand-wash them in the sink; otherwise, just toss them into the washing machine, wash on cold, and let them air-dry.

MATERIALS

100% cotton scrap fabric	*Scissors*
Iron	*Sewing pins*
Bowl or jar	*Sewing machine*
Ruler	*¼-inch-wide elastic cording*
Marking pencil	*Safety pin*

DIRECTIONS

1. Wash, dry, and iron the fabric. Lay the fabric flat on a table.

2. Choose the bowl or jar you want to make a cover for and lay it upside down on top of the fabric.

3. Mark a circle around the bowl approximately 2 inches wider than the circumference of the bowl. Cut out the circle.

4. Fold the edges of the fabric over approximately 1 inch to the wrong side of the fabric. This will form the casing for the elastic. As you fold it over, the casing will naturally form creases.

5. Pin the casing for sewing, being sure to include the creases. Iron the fold to make it easier to sew.

6. Using a straight stitch, sew along the border of the casing. Sew as close as possible to the edge of the fabric, leaving a 1- to 2-inch unstitched opening for the elastic.

7. To determine the length of the elastic, measure around the outside of the bowl 1 inch down from the lip of the bowl. Cut the elastic to length.

8. Attach a safety pin to one end of the elastic. Feed it through the casing, starting on one side of the opening.

9. Once you've pulled the elastic through the casing, overlap the elastic ends by approximately ¼ inch and sew them together 4 or 5 times.

10. Sew up the opening of the bowl cover and trim the excess thread.

MAKING AND TYING FUROSHIKI CLOTHS

Furoshiki is the Japanese art of wrapping and transporting objects. Not only does it offer a versatile and waste-free alternative to using disposable bags for carrying food, bottles, and other items, it's also a simple and sustainable way to wrap a gift. All that's needed is a square piece of cloth with finished edges. Beyond that, furoshiki cloths come in a wide range of sizes, materials, and patterns and can be tied in myriad ways using simple knots and folds. They're easy to make, but perhaps what I love most about furoshiki is that depending on what you need to wrap, you may be able to repurpose fabric scraps, old sheets, and other "knottable" fabric you can find in your personal fabric stash or local secondhand shop. To make a furoshiki cloth, simply cut your fabric into a square (the most popular size is 17 by 17 inches), finish the edges with your sewing machine or a pair of pinking shears, iron the finished cloth, and tie it according to one of the techniques below.

BASIC WRAP

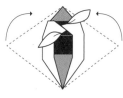

1. Place the object you want to wrap in the center of the furoshiki cloth.

2. Bring two opposite corners of the square to the center and tie in a knot.

3. Bring the remaining two opposite corners to the center and tie them in a knot above the first knot.

continued

BOTTLE WRAP

1. Stand a bottle in the center of the furoshiki cloth.

2. Bring two opposite corners of the square together above the bottle and tie a knot with the long ends.

3. Twist the long ends and then tie them in a knot above the first knot, to create a handle.

4. Tie the remaining two opposite corners in a knot at the front of the bottle.

HAND CARRY WRAP

1. Place the objects in the center of the furoshiki cloth.

2. Bring two corners on the same side together and tie them in a knot.

3. Bring the other two corners together and tie them in a knot.

4. Bring the two handles together to create a pouch that can be carried like a small handbag.

NEWSPAPER TRASH CAN LINERS

If composting is going well, I usually can go weeks without needing a plastic bin liner. The "wet" trash gets tossed in the compost bin and the dry trash goes into a 1-gallon trash can lined with newspapers. Once the liner is full, I put it in an outdoor trash can for curbside collection. You will need three sheets of newspaper.

DIRECTIONS

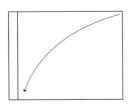 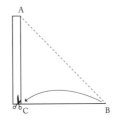 

1. Unfold and stack the newspaper sheets.

2. Fold one corner down to make a triangle. Cut off the excess strip of paper.

3. Fold point B to point C and make a crease.

4. Fold point A to points B and C and make a crease. You will have a square.

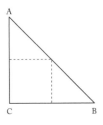 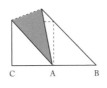

5. Unfold the last two creases so that you have a triangle again.

6. Fold point A to meet the midpoint of the opposite side. Point A will touch the start of the crease on that side.

7. Fold point B to meet the midpoint of the opposite side. Point B will touch the start of the crease on that side.

8. Separate the two sides (three layers each) at point C and fold each side down toward the bottom of the liner.

REDUCING HOUSEHOLD FOOD WASTE

According to Dana Gunders, author of the *Waste-Free Kitchen Handbook,* 40 percent of food in the United States goes uneaten, with the average American family of four throwing away the equivalent of up to $2,275 a year. On average, that comes out to 400 pounds of food per person every year. So where does it go? Unfortunately, to landfills, where it accounts for the single largest component of solid waste and a large portion of methane gas emissions. Although effective, large-scale solutions will require involvement from businesses and governments, there's plenty consumers can do to help. Indeed, the largest source of food waste is from households, which create more waste than grocery stores, restaurants, and almost any other part of the supply chain. Here are a few tips for reducing food waste at the household level.

MEAL PLAN AND SHOP WISELY. Create a meal plan, shop with a list, and avoid impulse purchases and marketing tricks that encourage you to buy things you don't need.

DECLUTTER AND TAKE INVENTORY BEFORE YOU SHOP. Keep your pantry, refrigerator, and freezer organized and tidy so it's easy to see what you have. Take inventory of your dried goods, fruits, veggies, and spices. If possible, clean out the fridge before you shop so you can figure out what you actually need. If you store your dried goods in clear glass jars and containers, it makes it easy to quickly take stock.

UNDERSTAND DATE LABELS. Treat expiration dates as guidelines rather than hard-and-fast rules. Sell-by date labels are not federally regulated; they're estimates from manufacturers for peak quality and freshness. Learn about spoilage indicators for specific foods so you can use your judgment to tell whether they're still edible before tossing.

BUY AND SERVE SMALL PORTIONS AND SAVE AND EAT LEFTOVERS. A significant source of household waste is attributed to large portions and uneaten leftovers. Be realistic when shopping, and buy only what you think you'll use. When cooking or eating in restaurants, serve or order small portions. Repurpose leftovers into new meals.

STORE FRUITS AND VEGETABLES CORRECTLY. Follow the tips on page 22 for storing fruits and vegetables to prolong their freshness and prevent spoilage.

USE THE FREEZER. Preserve and prevent spoilage by freezing foods. Almost everything can be frozen, including butter, cheese, meat, vegetables, fruits, nuts, and baked goods.

PREVENT SPOILAGE. Turn wilting or safe-but-aging produce and meat into freezable broths, sauces, or casseroles.

KEEP A STOCK JAR IN THE FREEZER. Add vegetable trimmings to a jar that you keep in the freezer. When it's full, prepare stock (see page 32).

FERMENT OR CAN FOODS. Learn old-fashioned ways of preserving fruits and vegetables, such as fermenting or canning them (see page 25).

SHARE FOOD. Share excess food—cooked, uncooked, or grown in your garden—with friends, family, coworkers, and neighbors. This helps prevent waste while building community.

BUY IMPERFECT PRODUCE. Support farmers, grocery stores, markets, and companies that sell imperfect produce. Buy so-called "ugly" fruits and vegetables that may look too small, too large, misshapen, bruised, or discolored but are otherwise safe and nutritious to eat.

COMPOST FOOD SCRAPS OR FEED THEM TO BACKYARD CHICKENS. Instead of tossing food scraps in the trash bin, consider composting them through a municipal composting program or using your own backyard system (see page 215). If you have backyard chickens, feed them scraps and let them help you reduce waste.

PRACTICE CLOSED-LOOP COOKING. Prevent food waste by using fruits and veggies, or parts of them, that are often overlooked and discarded. For example, use pulp left over from making juice to bake crackers (page 64) and carrot tops for pesto (page 248).

STORING FRUITS AND VEGETABLES

Here are a few guidelines for storing fruits and vegetables in a way that will extend their freshness without using plastic bags or wraps. You can invest in special storage materials like silicone storage bags, beeswax wraps, and fitted cloth covers, or you can use the containers and towels you already own.

Before jumping into the specifics of how to store each fruit and vegetable, it helps to know a little bit about your refrigerator. For optimal results, the temperature needs to be at or slightly below 40°F. Most refrigerators also have what are called crisper drawers, which are compartments designed for storing fruits and vegetables. Vegetables tend to do best in a high-humidity crisper, while fruits keep longer in a low-humidity environment. Many refrigerators have two separate compartments marked accordingly. If yours aren't marked, you can turn one drawer into a high-humidity drawer by making sure it's always closed tightly, and turn the other one into a low-humidity drawer by leaving it slightly ajar. To keep fruits and veggies for longer periods of time, they can also be preserved in the freezer (see page 25).

FRUITS

APPLES. Wash only when ready to use. Store on a cool counter for up to 2 weeks. For longer storage, place in the fridge.

AVOCADOS. Store on the counter. To stop ripening, place in the fridge.

BANANAS. Set on the counter at room temperature, away from other fruit. Once ripe, store in the fridge.

BERRIES. Wash only when ready to use. For blueberries, store in a covered bowl or container on a shelf in the refrigerator. For blackberries, raspberries, and strawberries, place in a single layer on a plate and store on a shelf in the refrigerator; stack the layers if necessary, but place a damp cloth between layers. Eat within a couple of days.

CHERRIES. Wash only when ready to eat. Most of the time they're sold ripe and should be refrigerated right away, in an airtight container.

CITRUS. Store loose in the low-humidity crisper drawer.

DATES. Place in an airtight container in the fridge.

FIGS. Wash only when ready to use. Store in an uncovered bowl on a shelf in the refrigerator.

GRAPES. Wash only when ready to use. Keep unwashed bunches in a paper bag on a shelf in the refrigerator.

MELONS. If unripe, store whole on the counter in a cool, dry place. Once ripe, store on a shelf in the refrigerator. If cut, refrigerate in an airtight container, regardless of ripeness.

PEARS. Wash only when ready to use. If firm and unripe, store on the counter. If soft and ripe, refrigerate in the low-humidity crisper drawer.

STONE FRUITS (APRICOTS, NECTARINES, PEACHES, PLUMS). Wash only when ready to use. If unripe, store on the counter at room temperature. If ripe, refrigerate in the low-humidity crisper drawer.

TROPICAL FRUITS (MANGOES, PAPAYAS, PINEAPPLES). If unripe, store whole on the counter at room temperature. Once ripe, store loose on a shelf in the refrigerator or in the low-humidity crisper drawer.

VEGETABLES

ASPARAGUS. Trim the ends and stand the stalks upright in a glass jar filled with 1 to 2 inches of water, or wrap in a damp cloth and store in the high-humidity crisper drawer.

BEETS. Remove the greens, leaving a 1-inch stem on the root. Store the roots and greens separately, in breathable produce bags in the high-humidity crisper drawer. Wash only when ready to use.

BROCCOLI. Wash only when ready to use. Store in the refrigerator in a breathable produce bag or wrap in a damp towel and store in the high-humidity crisper drawer.

CARROTS. Trim the greens, leaving a 1-inch stem attached. Store the carrots in a breathable bag in the high-humidty crisper drawer, or submerged in water in a sealed glass container. Store the greens in a breathable produce bag in the high-humidity crisper drawer. Wash only when ready to use.

CELERY. Trim the ends and stand the stalks upright in a glass jar filled with 1 to 2 inches of water on a shelf in the refrigerator or store in a breathable produce bag in the high-humidity crisper drawer.

CORN ON THE COB. Eat immediately, if possible—it doesn't stay fresh for long. If you can't eat it immediately, store it, still in the husks, in a wet paper bag inside a larger silicone bag in the high-humidity drawer.

CUCUMBER. Store on the counter or wrap in a damp cloth and store in a breathable produce bag in the high-humidity crisper drawer.

GARLIC. If unpeeled, store in a cool, dark place. If peeled, store in an airtight container in the refrigerator.

GINGER. Store loose or in an airtight container in the refrigerator.

GREEN BEANS AND PEAS. Store in a breathable produce bag in the high-humidity crisper drawer.

HEARTY GREENS. Wash only when ready to use. Remove any rubber bands, wrap in a damp towel, and store in the high-humidity crisper drawer.

HERBS. Prepare herbs (except basil) like a flower bouquet: Trim the stems and stand the sprigs in a glass of water; store in the refrigerator. Store basil in an airtight container, loosely packed with a damp cloth.

MUSHROOMS. Wash only when ready to use. Store in a paper bag in the high-humidity crisper drawer or on a lower shelf in the refrigerator.

ONIONS. Store in a cool, dark, well-ventilated area. Hanging sacks or baskets work well as they encourage ventilation. Keep away from potatoes—onions will encourage them to sprout!

PEPPERS. Store in a breathable produce bag in the low-humidity crisper drawer.

POTATOES AND WINTER SQUASH. Store in an open basket in a cold, dry, well-ventilated area. Store separately from onions.

SALAD GREENS. Wash only when ready to use. Store upright in a glass of water on the counter or wrap in a damp cloth and store in the high-humidity crisper drawer.

SUMMER SQUASH. Wash only when ready to use. Store in a breathable produce bag in the high-humidity crisper drawer in the refrigerator. Once cut, wrap in a damp towel and continue to store in the high-humidity drawer.

TOMATOES. If uncut, store on the counter at room temperature, away from sunlight. Once cut, store in the refrigerator for up to 3 days.

PRESERVING FOOD

When I was growing up, my grandmother prepared Sunday lunch every week for our entire extended family. As a little girl, I didn't appreciate it for what it was, but now it blows my mind. Not only did she host a whole herd of us, week after week, but she also made sure that at least some of the food she put on the table came from the backyard garden she kept with my grandfather. Their garden wasn't big by any stretch of the imagination, but she knew how to preserve her harvest in a way that made it seem like she had a midsize farm out back. Imagine eating creamed corn and bright green beans in December—we did!—and we had old-fashioned preservation methods to thank for it. My grandmother did a lot of freezing, which is the easiest way to put food by, while my great-grandmother relied more on canning, pickling, and fermentation.

People have been putting up food for millennia. Luckily, there are plenty of ways to preserve foods, and many of them are much easier than you might think. If you feel intimidated by the techniques and equipment that go with preserving, just remember that if you use a refrigerator or freezer—and I bet you do—you're already well on your way! That's because every time you put fresh produce, milk, eggs, or yogurt in the refrigerator, or last night's soup in the freezer to eat later in the month, you're practicing short-term preservation. Learning longer-term methods isn't much harder. If you zoom out a bit, you'll see that preserving is often simply a matter of packing veggies in a jar and covering them with brine, or bottling soup in glass jars and arranging them neatly in the freezer. Here's a short summary of some of the most common methods.

FREEZING. This is the easiest and most common way to prevent food waste and save it for another day. It's versatile, too—not only can freezing be used to preserve food for short- *or* long-term purposes, but there are also surprisingly few foods that don't freeze well. If you're putting something away just for a few days—say, leftovers you plan to eat later in the week—prep and storage are pretty straightforward. But if you plan to store something longer-term, there's a bit more involved than just popping it in a storage container and shelving it in the freezer. Here are a few tips:

- **BLANCH FRUITS AND VEGETABLES.** To help fruits and vegetables maintain their quality, it's best to blanch them before freezing. The process is simple: Cook in boiling water for 2 to 5 minutes, then submerge in an ice water bath to halt the cooking process. Since some foods take longer than others, the best technique is to taste the fruit or vegetables every 30 seconds to see if they're done. Simply remove one piece (a carrot or a green bean, for example), dip it into the bowl of ice water, and taste it. Keep tasting every 30 seconds until the fruit or vegetable is cooked to your liking.

- **FREEZE DELICATE FRUITS.** To keep berries from freezing together into a big icy clump, arrange them in a single layer on a rimmed baking sheet, place them in the freezer for an hour, then transfer them to a glass storage container or reusable silicone zip-top bag.

- **COLLECT SCRAPS FOR STOCK.** Keep a jar, paper bag, or silicone bag in the freezer to collect ingredients for stock. Toss in bones, onion peels, celery stalks, carrot trimmings, etc. Once you have enough, you can make a batch of stock (see page 32)—and freeze that, too.

- **USE THE RIGHT CONTAINERS.** If you're trying to avoid plastic, you can use mason jars, glass storage containers with plastic lids, and/or reusable silicone storage bags. Glass jars have a reputation for breaking easily in the freezer; to prevent breakage, use wide-mouth jars with straight (instead of tapered) shoulders; allow hot food to cool before ladling it into jars; leave 1 to 2 inches of headspace to allow for expansion; and cap the jar loosely until the food freezes, then seal it tightly.

- **PORTION WITH ICE CUBE TRAYS.** Ice cube trays provide a convenient way to freeze small portions of foods. Pour sauces, stock, pureed vegetables, or minced herbs in olive oil into ice cube trays, let them freeze, pop them out, and store the cubes in glass jars or silicone storage bags.

CANNING. In the process of home canning, food is placed in jars and heated (either on the stovetop or in a pressure canner) both to destroy harmful microorganisms that cause spoilage and to create an airtight seal that prevents contamination. Specific processing techniques, times, and temperatures are required according to the acidity of the food being preserved. The majority of common canned foods—like jams, jellies, pickles, tomatoes, and fruit—call for simple equipment you may already own: canning jars, two-piece metal closures, and a canner or large pot for holding and processing the jars. Low-acidity foods like most vegetables require a pressure canner. If you're interested in canning, I recommend starting with the water-boiler/stovetop method (and inviting a few friends to do it with you!). Properly home-canned foods can be stored in your cupboard for up to a year and are believed to be comparable in nutritional value to fresh vegetables.

PICKLING AND FERMENTING. Pickling and fermenting are ancient food preservation techniques. Pickling is a general term that can describe any method that preserves food by soaking it in an acidic solution. When most people refer to pickles, they mean cucumbers that have been soaked in vinegar. The kosher pickles you see on grocery store shelves are processed this way. Fermentation is a type of pickling that uses lactic acid as the acidic medium. In the process of fermentation, the starches and sugars in the food are converted into lactic acid by the bacteria lactobacilli. The lactic acid is what gives fermented foods their sour flavor. Similar to pickling, fermentation prevents the growth of bad bacteria; where it differs is that it also promotes the growth of good, healthy bacteria. In this sense, fermented foods are living foods, touted for their role in promoting digestive health. Examples of fermented foods include sauerkraut, kimchi, sourdough bread, kombucha, kefir, yogurt, and miso. Some pickles are also fermented. If you choose to buy fermented foods at the grocery store instead of making them yourself, make sure that they haven't been pasteurized, since doing so wipes out the cultures that will help fortify your gut. When it comes to fermenting fruits and vegetables, special equipment isn't necessary, but it sure makes it easier. No matter what, you'll need glass jars or ceramic crocks to hold the foods you want to ferment. You can also buy airlock lids to allow fermentation gases to escape and fermentation weights to keep foods submerged under brine, which helps prevent mold.

DEHYDRATING. Dehydrating or drying foods is one of the oldest and easiest ways to preserve foods. Removing water or moisture prevents the growth of bacteria, yeast, and molds and slows down enzymatic reactions that take place within food, both of which prevent food spoilage. Heat, dry air, and air movement are needed for success. Although many foods were originally dried in the sun, an oven or a dehydrator is safer, quicker, and easier. Generally speaking, the oven or dehydrator should be kept around 140°F. Although I'm not one to buy a lot of fancy and unnecessary kitchen equipment, I find my food dehydrator to be invaluable, especially in the summer when my garden is bursting with herbs practically begging to be harvested, dehydrated, and put away for tisanes, salves, tinctures, and other recipes and remedies.

CREATIVE USES FOR COFFEE GROUNDS

Coffee is good for more than just waking you up in the morning. Before you toss used grounds and send them to the landfill, consider putting them to use in the garden, around the house, or in bath and body products. Here are a few ways to repurpose them.

REPEL GARDEN PESTS. Sprinkle liberally around your plants or the perimeter of your garden to deter pests like ants, slugs, and snails.

ATTRACT WORMS. Work the grounds into your soil to attract these little garden helpers.

BOOST COMPOST. Add coffee grounds, along with the filter, directly to your compost pile. The grounds, which are rich in nitrogen, make excellent green matter.

FERTILIZE PLANTS. To make fertilizer, mix old grounds with dead grass clippings, brown leaves, or dry straw, then spread the mixture around acid-loving plants like azaleas, hydrangeas, rhododendrons, and roses.

JUMP-START CARROT AND RADISH SEEDS. To double your harvest, mix dried coffee grounds with carrot and radish seeds before planting them.

MAKE GARDENER'S SOAP. To make an exfoliating soap, melt one bar of glycerin soap, add ⅓ cup coffee grounds, mix well, and pour into a soap mold.

DEODORIZE YOUR FRIDGE. To neutralize food odors, fill a jar with grounds and place it, uncovered, at the back of the fridge.

DEODORIZE YOUR HANDS. After chopping garlic or onions, rub grounds on your hands to eliminate odors.

CLEAN TOOLS AND COOKWARE. Sprinkle coffee grounds onto a scrub brush and use them as an abrasive to remove stuck-on food from pots, pans, and utensils.

REMOVE PUFFINESS AND DARK CIRCLES UNDER EYES. Scoop up a little bit of cooled grounds with your fingers and apply to the area under your eyes. The caffeine constricts blood vessels, draws out excess moisture, and eliminates dark circles and bags.

REMOVE PRODUCT BUILDUP ON HAIR. Before shampooing, massage a handful of coffee grounds into your hair to remove residue from shampoo, conditioner, and other hair care products.

REPURPOSING EGGSHELLS

One food scrap that holds boundless potential for reuse is the eggshell. Here are a few of my favorite ways to use them.

DETER GARDEN PESTS. Sprinkle crushed eggshells around the garden to ward off slugs and snails. Grind them into a powder and sprinkle on plants to deter beetles.

BRIGHTEN WHITE LAUNDRY. Put eggshells in a mesh or muslin bag, secure tightly with string or twine, and add to the washing machine with a load of whites.

BOOST COMPOST. Toss eggshells into your compost pile to add calcium and other trace minerals to the mix.

FEED TO CHICKENS. Feed eggshells to your chickens as a calcium supplement. Let the eggshells dry out for a day or two, crush them, then mix them with the regular chicken feed.

BOOST INDOOR PLANTS. Fill a glass jar with crushed eggshells, top it with water, and soak for a few days. Strain and use the liquid to water houseplants.

START SEEDLINGS. Instead of pots, use eggshells as seedling starters. Poke holes in the bottom of eggshell halves, place them in an empty egg carton, fill each one with potting soil, and plant one or two seeds per shell.

FORTIFY GARDEN TOMATOES. To prevent blossom end rot in tomatoes, use a coffee grinder to crush eggshells into a fine powder that can be sprinkled in the hole before planting seeds or young tomato plants.

SCRUB POTS AND PANS. Mix crushed eggshells with hot water and use as an abrasive to scrub pots and pans. Rinse with soap and water to get completely clean.

USE IN VERMICOMPOSTING. Pulverize the eggshells, then feed them to your worms and use them to neutralize the pH of your bedding.

TREAT SKIN IRRITATIONS. Soak eggshells in a jar of apple cider vinegar for a couple of days, then use the solution to treat itchy skin and minor irritation.

USE IN ART PROJECTS. Dye white eggs different colors, then use the crushed shells to create mosaic artwork with glue, paint, and cardboard.

MAKE A SKIN-TIGHTENING FACE MASK. Combine 2 tablespoons of finely powdered eggshells with an egg white and mix into a paste. Apply as a natural face mask. Allow to dry for 15 to 20 minutes, then wash off with warm water, using circular motions to exfoliate.

FOOD SCRAP VEGGIE STOCK

Homemade vegetable stock is a great way to put veggie scraps and past-peak produce to use. As you're preparing vegetables throughout the week, wash and save the stalks, peels, and leaves and store them in a silicone bag, paper bag, or glass container. You can keep them in the refrigerator for up to a week; otherwise, to prevent spoilage, store them in the freezer. Once you have about 4 cups of scraps, you're ready to make stock. For depth and flavor, you can add beet greens, bell peppers, green beans, lettuce, mushrooms, parsnips, potato peels, scallions, squash, and Swiss chard. Vegetables that overpower and disappoint in a stock include artichokes, asparagus, broccoli, Brussels sprouts, cauliflower, rutabagas, and turnips. You should also avoid using beet roots unless you don't mind having a bright red stock! **Makes 2 quarts**

INGREDIENTS

1 tablespoon olive oil, coconut oil, or butter

2 large onions, chopped

2 medium carrots, chopped

3 celery ribs, chopped

1 leek, chopped

5 garlic cloves, chopped

8 cups water

4 cups vegetable scraps

A few fresh herb sprigs

Salt and pepper to taste

DIRECTIONS

In a large pot, heat the oil over medium heat. Add the onions, carrots, celery, leek, and garlic and sauté until tender. Add the water, vegetable scraps, and herbs and bring to a boil. Reduce to a simmer, partially cover, and continue to cook for about an hour. Pour the stock through a fine-mesh strainer into a large bowl and season with salt and pepper; compost the contents of the strainer. Allow the stock to cool, then transfer it to glass jars and store in the refrigerator or freezer. If you're freezing glass jars, avoid broken jars by allowing the stock to completely cool, using wide-mouth jars, leaving 1 to 2 inches of headspace to allow the stock to expand when it freezes, capping the jars loosely, and leaving a little space between the jars in the freezer.

SCRAP APPLE CIDER VINEGAR

Apple cider vinegar is a staple in the natural home. It can be used in baking, cooking, and cleaning as well as for concocting all manner of products for wellness and for bath and body care. When you use it as much as I do, it can start to get expensive and wasteful, particularly if you buy it raw and in quart-size glass containers. Fortunately, you can make it yourself for a fraction of the cost—or free if you choose to use apple scraps instead of new apples. I like to freeze cores as we eat apples and make a batch once I've saved enough for a quart or more of vinegar. This recipe makes 2 cups; feel free to double, triple, or quadruple it. **Makes 2 cups**

INGREDIENTS

3 cups chopped apples (from 2 whole apples; wash first and include the cores, stems, peels, and seeds)

2 tablespoons sugar (or 1 tablespoon per cup of filtered water)

2 cups filtered water, or enough to cover the apples

DIRECTIONS

1. Fill a clean, quart-size wide-mouth glass jar three-quarters of the way with the apple pieces. In a separate jar, dissolve the sugar in the filtered water. Pour the sugar water over the apples. Make sure they're completely submerged, pouring in a little more water if necessary. Use a fermentation weight (see page 241) to keep the apples submerged. Cover the jar with cheesecloth or a thin, breathable flour sack towel, secure it with a rubber band, and place the jar in a warm, dark place for 2 weeks. Gently mix the apples once a day to aerate the ferment, encourage microbial activity, and prevent mold. If brownish scum develops on top, skim it off with a spoon.

2. After 2 weeks, pour the liquid through a fine-mesh strainer into a clean wide-mouth glass jar. Compost the apple scraps. Cover the jar with a fresh piece of cheesecloth and secure it with a rubber band. Leave on the counter and allow it to ferment for 2 to 4 more weeks. You'll know it's ready when it smells and tastes tangy and acidic like vinegar. If it's not quite there, allow it to ferment for another week or two. Once you're happy with the taste, cap and store the vinegar in a cool, dark place until you're ready to use it. It will keep indefinitely.

FOOD SCRAP SIMMER POT

Instead of diffusing essential oils or burning seasonally scented candles, imagine creating a natural air freshener by simmering aromatic plants and food scraps in a pot of water. As the water simmers, not only does it make the whole house smell good, but it also adds warmth and moisture to the air, which is downright therapeutic during cold and flu season. Here is my favorite recipe for a fall simmer pot, but feel free to create your own blends using seasonal aromatics that complement one another. During the summer, I like to combine lemon peels, rosemary, and mint; for winter, I blend pine twigs, juniper berries, star anise, and nutmeg. The possibilities are endless!

INGREDIENTS

3 or 4 apple, orange, and/or lemon peels

3 drops vanilla extract or 1 vanilla bean

1 to 2 cinnamon sticks

2 to 4 star anise pods

1 fresh pine sprig

1 fresh rosemary sprig

1 cup dried lavender

2 tablespoons ground allspice

1 tablespoon whole cloves

½ teaspoon ground nutmeg

DIRECTIONS

Combine all the ingredients in a small pot and cover generously with water. Let simmer over low heat for up to 24 hours, adding water as needed to keep the ingredients submerged. Remove the pot from the heat when unattended for sleep or running errands. After 24 hours, strain the mixture and compost the scraps.

NOTE To save on energy, you can place the pot on top of a warm woodstove or radiator instead of using the kitchen stove.

NO-KNEAD ARTISAN BREAD

If you're new to making bread, this easy, no-knead recipe is the perfect place to start. It's made from four simple ingredients (plus some herbs, if you like) and requires no fancy equipment or techniques. It does require some waiting time—24 hours for it to rise and ferment—but your patience will be rewarded with a deliciously crusty bread, complete with a complex flavor and doughy interior. **Makes 1 loaf**

INGREDIENTS

3 cups all-purpose flour

1 teaspoon active dry yeast

2 teaspoons salt

1⅔ cups warm water (110°F)

1 tablespoon chopped fresh herbs (optional)

DIRECTIONS

1. In a large bowl, combine the flour, yeast, and salt. Gradually add the water and herbs (if using) and stir until blended. Mix the dough gently with your hands and mold it into a ball.

2. Cover the bowl with beeswax wrap and set aside to rise at room temperature for 18 to 24 hours. At the end of this period, the dough will be covered in bubbles.

3. Lightly flour a work surface and place the dough on it. Dust the dough with flour and fold it over on itself once or twice. Dust a kitchen towel with flour, place the dough on the floured towel, and cover it with another towel. Let the dough rise for 2 more hours. At the end of this period, the dough will have doubled in size.

4. About 30 minutes before the dough is ready, preheat the oven to 450°F. Place a lidded Dutch oven (or heavy-duty casserole dish) in the oven as it heats.

5. When the dough is ready, use a sharp knife to score an X into the top of the loaf. Each score mark should be about 2 inches long and ¼ inch deep.

6. Carefully remove the hot Dutch oven from the oven and place the dough in it. Cover and return to the oven to bake for 30 minutes. Remove the lid and bake for another 15 to 20 minutes, until the bread is golden brown on top.

7. Transfer the loaf to a wire rack and allow to cool for at least 30 minutes before serving.

HOMEMADE NUT MILK

While I appreciate the convenience of store-bought nut milk, there are lots of reasons to make it from scratch. First, you can buy just about any kind of nut from bulk bins, which means you can make a variety of different kinds of milk without creating waste. Homemade nut milk also tastes better, has fewer ingredients, and can be customized in a lot of different ways. If you make nut milk yourself, you have the option of soaking the nuts beforehand. Not only does this soften the nuts and draw out their rich flavors, it also neutralizes their phytic acid and enzyme inhibitors, which makes them easier to digest. Finally, if you make nut milk at home, you can use the leftover pulp to make crackers, hummus, truffles, and more. So before you toss the pulp, be sure to check out the recipes following this one. **Makes 4 cups**

INGREDIENTS

1 cup raw, unsalted almonds, cashews, hazelnuts, macadamia nuts, pecans, pistachios, or walnuts

3 cups water for soaking the nuts

Kosher salt (see chart)

4 cups water for blending

Honey or maple syrup (optional)

DIRECTIONS

Put the nuts in a medium bowl and cover with the 3 cups water. Add the salt, cover the bowl with a cloth, and let soak at room temperature for 8 to 12 hours. Drain and rinse the nuts with cool water. Transfer the nuts to a blender and add the 4 cups water. Blend on high speed until the nuts are broken down into a fine meal and the liquid is opaque. Using a nut milk bag or cheesecloth, strain the milk into a large bowl. Squeeze the bag to release as much milk as possible. Add honey or maple syrup to taste and store the milk in an airtight jar in the refrigerator for up to 4 days.

SALT MEASUREMENTS FOR SOAKING NUTS (PER CUP)

ALMONDS	¾ teaspoon	PECANS	½ teaspoon
CASHEWS	¾ teaspoon	PISTACHIOS	no soaking required
HAZELNUTS	¾ teaspoon	WALNUTS	½ teaspoon
MACADAMIA NUTS	¾ teaspoon		

ALMOND PULP CRACKERS

You can customize these crackers to your liking by using any of your favorite seeds, herbs, or spices. **Makes approximately 2 dozen crackers**

INGREDIENTS

*1 cup firmly packed almond pulp
(left over from homemade nut milk, page 40)*

1 tablespoon ground flax seeds

1 tablespoon sesame seeds

*1 tablespoon finely chopped
fresh flat-leaf parsley (optional)*

*1 teaspoon dried basil, oregano, sage,
or thyme*

1 garlic clove, minced

¼ teaspoon sea salt

3 tablespoons olive oil

DIRECTIONS

1. Preheat the oven to 275°F.

2. Combine the almond pulp, seeds, herbs, garlic, and salt in the bowl of a food processor and process until smooth. Transfer the dough to a bowl and add the olive oil. Mix well. Use your hands to roll the dough into a ball, then place it between two sheets of compostable parchment paper. Using a rolling pin, roll the dough out to an even ¼-inch thickness. Remove the top sheet of parchment, then use a knife or pizza cutter to cut the dough into 1- to 2-inch squares. Gently transfer the parchment paper with the crackers to a baking sheet.

3. Bake for 20 minutes, then flip the crackers and bake for another 15 to 20 minutes, until crisp. Let cool completely before serving. Store in an airtight container at room temperature for up to a week.

NUT PULP CHOCOLATE TRUFFLES

Here's a great use for leftover pulp after making nut milk—and the perfect way to pack in some protein while appeasing your sweet tooth. **Makes 12 to 15 truffles**

INGREDIENTS

$1\frac{1}{4}$ cups nut pulp (left over from homemade nut milk, page 40)

$\frac{1}{2}$ cup desiccated coconut (optional)

$\frac{1}{4}$ cup cacao powder

$\frac{1}{4}$ cup raw honey

1 teaspoon vanilla extract

1 teaspoon ground cinnamon

Pinch sea salt

Toppings: ground cinnamon, coconut flour, and/or cocoa powder (about $\frac{1}{2}$ cup total)

DIRECTIONS

Combine all the ingredients except the toppings in a blender and blend until smooth. Roll the dough into bite-size balls. Roll the balls in the topping(s) of your choice. Serve immediately or store in an airtight container in the refrigerator for up to 4 days.

FRESH COCONUT MILK

If you're looking for a nondairy alternative to cow's milk, coconut milk is a wonderful option. It's great for the brain, supplies the body with a quick boost of energy, and is antiviral, antimicrobial, and antibacterial. Although it can be purchased from the grocery store in a carton or a can, if you have access to fresh coconuts, you can also make it from scratch. It might feel a bit labor-intensive the first time you make it, but once you get the hang of it, and after you experience the taste of fresh, creamy coconut milk, you may never go back to buying the store-bought stuff. If you're really into zero-waste, you'll also love that the only thing you have to toss is the coconut shell, and it can go right into the compost pile! **Makes about 2 cups**

INGREDIENTS

1 fresh coconut   *1½ cups hot water*

DIRECTIONS

1. Using a sharp knife, pierce the softest eye of the coconut and drain the liquid into a medium bowl.

2. Place the coconut on a hard surface and look for the imperfect "equator" line that runs along the middle of the coconut. With a hammer, whack along the equator line until the coconut cracks open.

3. Using your fingers, pry apart the two halves of the coconut and place them cut side down. Tap the back sides of the coconut halves with a hammer to loosen the meat from the shell; it's okay if the shell breaks. Slide a butter knife between the coconut shell and the meat and pry the meat away from each piece. Peel off any brown bits of skin that stick to the coconut meat. Chop the meat into ½- to ¾-inch pieces; you will need 1 cup.

4. Combine the coconut liquid, chopped coconut meat, and hot water in a blender and blitz until smooth, then strain through cheesecloth. (Using hot water will help draw out oil from the coconut and create a thicker milk.)

5. Use the milk right away, if possible; otherwise, transfer it to a glass jar with an airtight lid and store for up to 3 days in the refrigerator.

COCONUT FLOUR

If you've just made your first batch of fresh coconut milk (page 44), you might be wondering what to do with the leftover coconut pulp. Simple: Make coconut flour! It blends well with nut flours to make a variety of gluten- and grain-free baked goods, and it's a great source of fiber. You can use your oven or a food dehydrator, if you have one. **Makes approximately ½ cup**

INGREDIENTS

Fresh coconut pulp (left over from fresh coconut milk, page 44), about 1 cup

DIRECTIONS

1. If you're using an oven, preheat it to 150°F (or the lowest temperature setting possible).

2. Spread the pulp on a rimmed baking sheet lined with compostable parchment paper or on the nonstick sheet of a food dehydrator. Dehydrate the pulp in the oven for about 4 to 5 hours, until dry but not browned, or in the dehydrator at 90°F for about 1 hour.

3. Transfer the dried pulp to a blender and blend for about a minute.

4. Store in an airtight container at room temperature.

COCONUT YOGURT

If you have some leftover fresh coconut meat (not to be confused with pulp; see the recipe on page 44 for more about fresh coconut, including how to open it), you can use it to make coconut yogurt. You'll just need two high-quality probiotic capsules to jump-start the process and a couple of days' worth of patience. Not only is fresh coconut yogurt delicious, it's also a great way to minimize waste by avoiding plastic yogurt cups. If additives aren't your thing, you'll appreciate that making it yourself allows you to control the ingredients, choose your favorite sweetener, and avoid fillers and preservatives. **Makes approximately 2 cups**

INGREDIENTS

2 cups chopped coconut meat (from 2 fresh coconuts)

¼ to ½ cup coconut water or filtered water

2 probiotic capsules

Honey or maple syrup (optional)

DIRECTIONS

Combine the coconut meat and coconut water in a blender and blend until smooth and creamy. Pour the mixture through a fine-mesh strainer into a clean, wide-mouth glass jar. Open the probiotic capsules and empty the contents into the jar. Stir with a wooden spoon or popsicle stick (avoid using metal utensils as they can deactivate the probiotics). Cover the jar with cheesecloth or a thin, breathable kitchen towel and secure it with a rubber band. Allow the coconut milk to ferment at room temperature for 24 to 72 hours. The longer you leave it to ferment, the tangier it will be. If you live in a cold climate, you can put the jar in the oven and turn on the light (but not the oven!). The light will provide just enough heat to allow the bacteria from the probiotics to do their work. Once the yogurt is fermented, sweeten it with honey or maple syrup if you like. Cap the jar and store the yogurt in the fridge for up to 1 week.

WASTE-FREE HUMMUS

One of the best ways to cut down on plastic packaging is to prepare food from scratch. A good place to start is with staples like dips, condiments, and salad dressings. In our house, we eat a lot of hummus, so naturally it was one of the first staples I learned to make myself. Although you can make low-waste hummus using a BPA-free can of chickpeas, you can also make it the zero-waste way by using dried chickpeas from bulk bins. If you want to cook extra beans to use for salads and snacks, they'll keep in the refrigerator for up to 5 days. Otherwise, you can freeze them with or without liquid in glass jars. **Makes 1½ cups**

INGREDIENTS

½ cup dried chickpeas (1½ cups cooked)

2 tablespoons tahini, store-bought or homemade (page 51)

1 tablespoon lemon juice, plus more as needed

1 garlic clove, peeled

¼ teaspoon sea salt

¼ cup olive oil

DIRECTIONS

1. Put the chickpeas in a medium bowl or quart-size glass jar, pour in enough water to cover by 2 inches, cover with a plate or towel, and set aside to soak overnight.

2. Drain and rinse the chickpeas, then transfer them to a heavy-bottomed pot. Pour in enough fresh water to cover them by 2 inches and bring to a boil over medium-high heat. Reduce the heat to a low simmer, cover, and cook until tender, approximately 45 minutes.

3. Strain the chickpeas, reserving the liquid, and allow to cool. Once cooled, remove the skins from the chickpeas (this is tedious but worth it for the best texture).

4. To make the hummus, combine the cooked chickpeas, tahini, lemon juice, garlic, and salt in the bowl of a food processor. Process until smooth and creamy, 3 to 5 minutes. Slowly pour in the olive oil and continue to process until all the oil is mixed in. Taste and adjust the flavor and consistency with lemon juice, salt, or chickpea liquid. Transfer to an airtight container and store in the refrigerator for up to 1 week.

TAHINI FROM SCRATCH

When I started making hummus from scratch, I didn't consider making my own tahini. I figured I'd need special equipment to prepare and process it. As it turns out, it's very easy to make—all you need are two simple ingredients and a food processor. The benefits of making it yourself are fairly obvious: You save money and avoid wasteful packaging by not having to buy it prepared at the grocery store, *and* you prevent food waste by making small batches according to your needs. There *is* a secret to making good-tasting tahini though, and I think it's in using hulled seeds and being extra careful not to over-toast them. When toasting the sesame seeds, aim for a light golden color and do everything in your power not to let them brown. You can also skip toasting them altogether, but I find that toasting them slightly enhances the flavor and reduces the bitterness of the seeds. **Makes approximately ½ cup**

INGREDIENTS

1 cup hulled sesame seeds   *Salt (optional)*

2 to 4 tablespoons neutral-flavored oil
(such as grapeseed or olive)

DIRECTIONS

Put the seeds in a skillet and toast over low to medium heat for 3 to 5 minutes, stirring constantly to prevent burning. Remove the pan from the heat as soon as the seeds turn golden. Pour the seeds onto a rimmed baking sheet, spread them out, and allow them to cool for 20 minutes. Transfer the seeds to the bowl of a food processor and process until a crumbly paste forms. Scrape down the sides of the food processor and slowly add the oil, 1 tablespoon at a time. Continue to blend and add oil until the tahini is smooth and pourable. Add salt to taste, and store in an airtight container in the refrigerator for up to a month. If the sesame paste and oil separate over time, just give the tahini a good stir before using.

Top left: Waste-Free Hummus (page 49); top right: Tahini from Scratch (above);
bottom left: Homemade Ketchup (page 53); bottom right: Homemade Nut Butter (page 59)

PACKAGE-FREE GUACAMOLE

Like hummus, guacamole is one of those dips you see conveniently packaged and sold in grocery stores. To save money and prevent waste, I recommend finding a good recipe and learning to make it yourself. It takes all of 3 minutes and results in a fresh and delicious side dish that beats the store-bought stuff any day of the week. To prevent food waste and keep your guacamole from turning brown, you can either eat it immediately or try this clever hack: Put the guacamole in a glass storage container, cut an onion in half, place the cut side of the onion down on the surface of the guacamole, and seal the container with an airtight lid. (Covering the surface of the guac with plastic wrap works best, but since we're trying to avoid plastic, the onion is a great alternative.) **Makes approximately 2½ cups**

INGREDIENTS

3 ripe avocados, halved and pitted

¼ cup diced red onion

¼ cup chopped fresh cilantro

1 small jalapeño, seeds and ribs removed, diced

Zest and juice of 2 limes

½ teaspoon coarse sea salt, plus more to taste

½ teaspoon ground cumin

DIRECTIONS

In a medium-size bowl, combine all of the ingredients. Mash with a fork until they are well combined but still chunky. Taste and adjust the seasoning with additional lime juice and salt, as needed. Serve immediately or store in an airtight container in the refrigerator for up to 2 days.

NOTE If you have a ripe, in-season tomato, you can seed it, dice it, and add it to this recipe.

HOMEMADE KETCHUP

Ketchup is one of those all-American foods I could easily live without. However, I'm the mother of two young children who—like many of their little counterparts—will eat just about anything if you put ketchup on it. Ketchup on its face isn't really a problem—unless you're trying to reduce disposable waste and avoid sugar. Try to find a glass bottle of ketchup without processed sugar—it's not easy! But fortunately, healthy, package-free ketchup isn't all that hard to make. **Makes 3 cups**

INGREDIENTS

3 pounds Roma tomatoes, skinned, seeded, and chopped

1/3 cup diced onion

1 garlic clove, minced

1/4 cup apple cider vinegar, store-bought or homemade (page 34)

1 teaspoon prepared mustard

1/4 teaspoon Worcestershire sauce

2 teaspoons sea salt

1/2 teaspoon black peppercorns

1/4 teaspoon allspice berries

1/4 teaspoon ground cinnamon

1 bay leaf

2 tablespoons raw honey, or to taste

DIRECTIONS

Combine all the ingredients except the honey in a medium pot and bring to a boil over medium heat. Reduce the heat and simmer for 30 to 45 minutes, until the tomatoes have begun to break down and release their juices. Remove the pot from the heat and allow to cool. Remove and discard the bay leaf, then use an immersion blender or countertop blender to puree the mixture. Stir in the honey and store in an airtight container in the refrigerator for up to 2 weeks or freeze for later.

MUSTARD TWO WAYS: SLOW AND QUICK

You can make homemade mustard the old-fashioned, slow way or the new-and-improved, quick way. I suggest trying both to see which one you like best. The old-fashioned recipe definitely has a kick to it—so much so that I like to add a little honey to help round it out. The quick mustard reminds me of the kind you find at every hot dog stand in America, and is probably better suited to a child's palate (unless you have one of those children that will eat anything). I'm often able to find mustard seeds and mustard powder in the bulk section of my grocery store; otherwise, both ingredients can be found in the spice aisle of most grocery stores.

SLOW MUSTARD

Makes 1½ cups

INGREDIENTS

½ cup yellow mustard seeds

½ cup water

½ cup apple cider vinegar, store-bought or homemade (page 34)

4 teaspoons fresh lemon juice

1 teaspoon honey, or more to taste

2 teaspoons paprika

1 teaspoon ground turmeric

1 teaspoon sea salt

DIRECTIONS

In a clean quart-size glass jar, combine the mustard seeds, water, and apple cider vinegar. Mix well, seal, and let sit at room temperature for 2 to 3 days. Add the lemon juice, honey, paprika, turmeric, and salt and use an immersion blender or a countertop blender to puree until smooth. If it is too thick, add warm water, 1 teaspoon at a time, until it has the right consistency. Transfer to a glass jar and store in the refrigerator for up to 1 month.

QUICK MUSTARD

Makes approximately 1 cup

INGREDIENTS

1 cup mustard powder

1½ teaspoons salt

½ teaspoon garlic powder

½ teaspoon ground turmeric

¼ teaspoon paprika

1 cup water

¾ cup apple cider vinegar, store-bought or homemade (page 34)

DIRECTIONS

In a medium saucepan, mix the mustard powder, salt, garlic powder, turmeric, and paprika. Add the water and apple cider vinegar and whisk until smooth. Bring to a boil over medium-high heat, then reduce the heat to a low simmer and cook, stirring constantly, for 5 to 10 minutes, until it has the consistency of mustard. Remove the pan from the heat and allow the mustard to cool for 15 minutes. Transfer to an airtight container and store in the refrigerator for up to 1 month. The mustard will be a bit pungent for the first few days but will mellow with time.

EVERYDAY SALAD DRESSINGS

Growing up, I remember half the refrigerator taken up by containers of condiments and salad dressings. I'm not sure why we needed so many, but I often think it's because my mother felt overwhelmed by all the choices at the grocery store. As an adult, I avoid the salad dressing aisle entirely. For one thing, there really are too many options. And second, I feel disappointed that even the so-called healthy brands sometimes include rancid oils and refined sugars. Fortunately, it's easy to make your own dressings—and some of the lightest and best-tasting ones are made from ingredients you probably keep stocked in your cupboards and spice cabinet. This first dressing is my go-to when I want something light; the lemon tahini (page 58) is my favorite when I want something more filling. For the simple vinaigrette, you can use store-bought or homemade apple cider vinegar (page 34), or vinegar of four thieves (page 259).

SIMPLE VINAIGRETTE

Makes about 1 cup

INGREDIENTS

3 tablespoons fresh lemon juice or vinegar

1 teaspoon prepared mustard

1 or 2 garlic cloves, minced

Chopped fresh herbs (optional)

$\frac{1}{2}$ teaspoon sea salt

$\frac{1}{4}$ teaspoon freshly cracked pepper

$\frac{3}{4}$ cup olive oil

DIRECTIONS

In a bowl, whisk together the lemon juice, mustard, garlic, herbs (if using), salt, and pepper. Slowly add the olive oil and whisk continuously to emulsify. Transfer to an airtight container and store in the refrigerator for up to 1 week. Shake well to re-emulsify before serving.

continued

LEMON TAHINI DRESSING

Makes about 1¼ cups

INGREDIENTS

*½ cup tahini, store-bought
or homemade (page 51)*

⅔ cup filtered water, plus more if needed

3 tablespoons fresh lemon juice

1 tablespoon olive oil

3 or 4 fresh cilantro sprigs, chopped

1 garlic clove, peeled

⅛ teaspoon ground cumin

Salt and ground black pepper, to taste

DIRECTIONS

Combine the tahini, water, lemon juice, olive oil, cilantro, garlic, and cumin in a blender and blend until smooth and creamy. Add more water, 1 teaspoon at a time, if needed to achieve your preferred consistency. Taste and season with salt and pepper. Use immediately or transfer to an airtight container and store in the refrigerator for up to 1 week. Shake well to re-emulsify before serving.

HOMEMADE NUT BUTTER

Making homemade nut butter is a simple affair: It requires as little as one ingredient (nuts!), involves two simple steps, and takes less than 30 minutes. The benefits include saving money, controlling the quality of your ingredients, and reducing packaging and food waste by buying just what you need from bulk bins. The hardest step is choosing your base—you can use one type of nut or a combination of two or more varieties. Any nut will work, including almonds, pecans, walnuts, hazelnuts, macadamia nuts, or cashews. If you're allergic to nuts, seeds such as sunflower, pumpkin, or sesame will work, too. Peanuts, which are technically a legume, are obviously a popular choice. Aside from combining different nuts and seeds to create a variety of flavors, you can also experiment with some of the suggested add-ins below. Be careful not to add maple syrup or honey to your base, as it can change the consistency of the nut butter. If you're looking to make it sweet, it's best to add these sweeteners with each serving of your nut butter. **Makes 2 cups**

INGREDIENTS

4 cups raw or sprouted nuts or seeds

Add-ins (optional): sea salt, vanilla extract, ground cinnamon, coconut butter, and/or chocolate chips

DIRECTIONS

1. Preheat the oven to 300°F.

2. Spread the nuts in a single layer on a rimmed baking sheet and roast for 8 to 12 minutes, until fragrant and slightly brown. Let cool. If using hazelnuts, remove and discard the skins.

3. Transfer the nuts to a food processor or high-speed blender and blend on high speed until the nuts are finely ground. Although you might be tempted to add oil or water at this stage, don't—the oils will eventually come out of the nuts and form a creamy paste. Instead, scrape down the sides of the blender or food processor and continue to blend the nuts into a creamy butter. This can take 10 to 15 minutes, depending on the fat content of the nuts. Once the nut butter is creamy, incorporate your add-ins, if desired, then transfer the nut butter to an airtight container and store in the refrigerator for up to 1 month.

ZERO-WASTE SNACK IDEAS

One thing I like about zero-waste is that it lends itself to eating simply and healthfully. My family tends to snack on fresh fruits and vegetables, but when we need a little more variety, we head to the bulk bins or I bake something special. Below are some zero-waste snack ideas, followed by a few simple recipes.

APPLE OR BANANA SLICES TOPPED WITH NUT BUTTER. For a more decadent snack, drizzle with honey and sprinkle with chocolate chips.

ANTS ON A LOG. Remember these old-fashioned snacks? Just cut celery in 3-inch pieces, fill with nut butter, and top with raisins.

BULK POPCORN. Homemade popcorn is the best! It requires no special equipment—just a pot with a lid—and you can season it however you like: with coconut oil, olive oil, nutritional yeast, grated Parmesan, sea salt, herbal salt, ground cumin, curry powder, ground turmeric, or ground cinnamon.

CRUDITÉS WITH HOMEMADE HUMMUS OR GUACAMOLE. Just use my recipes for hummus (page 49) and guacamole (page 52) and serve with cut-up carrots, celery, cucumbers, and bell peppers.

DRIED FRUIT. If you have a dehydrator, you can dry fruits when they're in season; otherwise, head to the bulk bins. Our favorites are apple rings, banana chips, cherries, dates, figs, mangoes, pineapples, and raisins.

TRAIL MIX. You can usually find a variety of different trail mixes in the bulk bins or make your own by combining your favorite nuts, seeds, dried fruits, and chocolate.

GRANOLA. You can make your own or buy one of the varieties in the bulk aisle. It can be eaten plain or as a topping for yogurt or as cereal with nut milk.

HARD-BOILED EGGS. I usually boil half a dozen eggs on Sundays and give them to my children for quick snacks throughout the week. They travel well, too.

SMOOTHIES. If berries are in season (or if you froze them in the summer), smoothies are an easy zero-waste snack. My favorite basic recipe is 1 cup frozen strawberries, 1 frozen banana, and the juice of 2 oranges. You can add nut butter, nut milk, or an avocado for some protein and healthy fats.

SALTY BULK FOOD SNACKS. There are endless options for premade salty bulk snacks, including plantain chips, pretzels, wasabi peas, rice crackers, and sesame sticks.

DRIED APPLE RINGS

Dehydrating fruit is a great way to preserve seasonal produce without having to use your freezer. It's also a great way to save money: You don't have to shell out for pricey bags of dried fruit, and the raw produce is less expensive when it's in season. Making dried apple rings is so easy and the result so flavorful that it has become a seasonal tradition for me. Here I share two ways to make them: with or without a dehydrator. **Makes approximately 1 gallon (or about 100 rings)**

INGREDIENTS

5 pounds apples

1 quart filtered water (optional)

¼ cup fresh lemon juice (optional)

3 tablespoons ground cinnamon (optional)

DIRECTIONS

1. Wash, core, and peel the apples. Using a sharp knife, a mandoline, or an old-fashioned apple slicer, slice the apples as thinly as possible, about ¼ inch thick. If you wish to keep the apples from browning, combine the filtered water and lemon juice in a medium bowl and let the apples soak for 30 minutes. Otherwise, proceed to step 2. Drain the apple slices and pat them dry with cloth napkins or towels.

2. If using a dehydrator, spread out the apple slices in a single layer on food dehydrator trays. If you wish, sprinkle with the cinnamon. Dehydrate at 135°F for 6 to 8 hours.

3. If using an oven, preheat it to 150°F (or the lowest temperature setting possible). Spread out the apple slices in a single layer on wire baking or cooling racks. If you wish, sprinkle with the cinnamon. Place the racks in the oven. Close the oven door, propping it slightly open to allow for air circulation. Bake for 5 to 8 hours, depending on your oven, the thickness of the apples, and the apple variety.

4. Remove the apples from the dehydrator or oven and check to see if they are completely dry on both sides as well as inside. The apples should feel leathery. If not, keep drying them until they are done.

5. Let cool for a few hours, then store in an airtight jar in a cool, dark place for up to 6 months.

VEGGIE JUICE PULP CRACKERS

If you use a juicer, you've probably wondered what to do with all that leftover veggie pulp. While you could certainly compost it, you can also use it to make these delicious crackers. They work best in the food dehydrator at 160°F, but you can also dehydrate them in an oven at the lowest setting. I like using carrot juice pulp best, but pulp from greens works well, too. **Makes 12 crackers**

INGREDIENTS

1 cup flax seeds

⅔ cup water

½ cup almond flour, plus more if needed

¼ cup pulp left over from making veggie juice, plus more if needed

¼ cup pumpkin seeds

Salt to taste

DIRECTIONS

1. Put the flax seeds in a medium bowl, cover with the water, and let soak for 1 hour.

2. If using an oven, preheat it to 150°F (or the lowest temperature setting possible).

3. Add the almond flour, veggie pulp, pumpkin seeds, and salt to the flax mixture and roll into a ball. If the mixture seems too wet, add more almond flour; if it seems too dry, add more pulp. Transfer the dough ball to a sheet of compostable parchment paper. Place another sheet of parchment on top. Using a rolling pin, flatten out the dough to about ¼ inch thick. Remove the top sheet of parchment and cut the dough into cracker-size pieces.

4. Transfer the crackers to a dehydrator (set at 160°F) or place the sheet of parchment with the crackers on a rimmed baking sheet in the oven. Cook for about 6 hours, or overnight, until dry and crisp. Let cool, then store in an airtight container at room temperature for up to a week.

CRISPY CHICKPEAS

These are a favorite healthy snack. You can either start with dried chickpeas, soaking and cooking them as you would to make hummus (page 49), or use chickpeas from a can. Either way, they're low-waste, versatile, and absolutely delicious. I like to season them with ground turmeric, cumin, and ginger, but other options include chili powder, curry powder, paprika, and/or chopped oregano, rosemary, and thyme. **Makes 1½ cups**

INGREDIENTS

One 15-ounce can chickpeas, rinsed, drained, and patted very dry (or 1½ cups cooked chickpeas, if starting from dried)

2 tablespoons olive oil

3 to 4 teaspoons ground spices or chopped herbs, fresh or dried

Kosher salt and ground black pepper

DIRECTIONS

1. Preheat the oven to 400°F. Line a rimmed baking sheet with compostable parchment paper.

2. Spread the chickpeas evenly on the prepared baking sheet. Roast until golden and crispy, 20 to 25 minutes. Turn off the oven and let the chickpeas bake for another 5 to 10 minutes.

3. Meanwhile, heat the oil in a small saucepan over medium heat. Add the spices or herbs, mix well, and cook for 1 minute. Remove the pan from the heat, add the chickpeas, and toss to coat with the flavored oil. Season with salt and pepper and serve, or cool and store in an airtight container at room temperature for 3 to 4 days.

NATURAL
CLEANING

Ingredient labels are mandatory for food, cosmetics, and drugs sold in the United States, but not for cleaning products. In a 2012 study of more than two thousand cleaning products, the Environmental Working Group (EWG) found that only 7 percent of cleaning products adequately disclosed their contents; others either failed to list ingredients, disclosed only a few ingredients, or described ingredients in vague terms such as "surfactant" or "solvent." The study found that 53 percent of cleaning products assessed contained ingredients that harm the lungs, 22 percent contained ingredients that cause asthma, and many others were formulated or contaminated with carcinogens or hormone disrupters.

I didn't have access to the EWG's report when I was pregnant with my first child. Even if I had, I probably would have done just as much hand-wringing to figure out what products were safe to use around a baby. Shopping for "green" products wasn't easy. The cleaning supplies industry was (and still is) "awash" with greenwashing, and I didn't have the time or patience to investigate what companies really meant when they claimed to use "nontoxic," "biodegradable," and "earth-friendly" ingredients. In the end I handed over a wad of cash for expensive cleaners sold at my natural grocery store and hoped for the best.

A few years later, when I got bitten by the zero-waste bug, I began scrutinizing my cleaning supplies again. This time, in addition to eliminating toxic ingredients, I was resolute in wanting to avoid disposable packaging.

What I discovered is that you can keep your home clean without putting people or the planet at risk, and the easiest and cheapest way to do that is to make your cleaning products yourself. Homemade products made from simple ingredients have been keeping homes clean for generations. My own grandmother, a meticulous homemaker, relied on nothing more than vinegar, baking soda, lemon, and salt. When I was in the Peace Corps, my host mother in Guinea made her mud hut sparkle with little more than soap, water, and elbow grease.

When I think about these women, I am also inspired by the simple tools they used to clean their homes. Built to last, these tools were made from natural, sustainable materials like wood and straw. In Guinea, my host mother used a simple broom made from twigs, reeds, and grasses that she tied together with twine. My grandmother cleaned with reusable towels, a wooden-handled corn broom, and a simple cotton string mop.

These two women were my role models as I transitioned to a zero-waste mindset and lifestyle. I've found that a natural cleaning routine is not only healthier for me and the planet, but it's empowering and joyful as well. In this section, I share the recipes and tools I use, and I hope they bring you joy and peace of mind. Done right, these methods can help save money, decrease your exposure to toxins often found in commercial products, and reduce your carbon footprint.

NATURAL CLEANING SUPPLIES

Here they are: the only supplies you'll ever need to keep your home clean. Most of these items can be readily purchased in cardboard or glass packaging at a grocery store, hardware store, or pharmacy. Some supplies, like hydrogen peroxide and castile soap, come in plastic bottles unless you have access to a zero-waste store. Even still, by making your own cleaning supplies, you'll cut down on packaging considerably since most of the recipes in this section call for small quantities of these ingredients. I can usually make a bottle of hydrogen peroxide last for 6 months! In the name of zero-waste and conserving resources, I suggest using up the supplies you have unless you're pregnant or allergic to them. If you choose to toss them, be sure to contact your local government for advice on how to dispose of them. Avoid emptying commercial cleaning products down drains or flushing them down toilets, as many of their ingredients aren't easily filtered by water treatment plants.

BAKING SODA (SODIUM BICARBONATE). Versatile and slightly alkaline, this pantry staple can be used to clean, deodorize, scour, polish, soften water, cut grease, and remove stains.

BEESWAX OR CANDELILLA WAX. Combines well with olive oil or coconut oil to make wood butter for polishing furniture.

CITRIC ACID. Removes soap scum, hard water stains, calcium deposits, lime, and rust.

CORNSTARCH. Can be used to clean windows, polish furniture, and shampoo carpets and rugs.

DISTILLED WHITE VINEGAR. Cuts grease and removes tarnish, odors, soap scum, mineral deposits, stains, and wax buildup. Inhibits the growth of mold, mildew, and bacteria.

ESSENTIAL OILS. Can disinfect and add a safe, natural fragrance to most cleaners. Tea tree, lemon, and eucalyptus are powerful antibacterials; lavender, rose, and geranium promote a sense of calm.

HYDROGEN PEROXIDE (3%). A weak acid with strong oxidizing properties; useful for bleaching and removing stains; as a disinfectant, can be used to sanitize surfaces, knobs, handles, and toilets.

LEMONS. One of the strongest food acids; cuts grease, disinfects and sanitizes, bleaches and removes stains, and makes a wonderful scouring paste when mixed with salt.

LIQUID CASTILE SOAP. Gentle, plant-based soap; removes grime and dirt.

OLIVE OIL OR COCONUT OIL. Make great wood polishers; can be used to oil hinges, remove labels, buff streaks on stainless steel, dust, and clean residue, gum, and paint from surfaces and materials.

RUBBING ALCOHOL. Kills germs, as well as mildew and mold; can be used to shine chrome and glass.

SAL SUDS (DR. BRONNER'S). A tougher version of castile soap (technically a detergent); cleans tougher grime and dirt.

SALT. Makes a great addition to any scouring paste, softens hard water and clothes, pulls stains from fabrics and carpets, and can be used as a natural scent booster.

VODKA. Serves as an effective disinfectant especially because of its high alcohol content, lack of scent, and absence of color. In general, the higher the proof, the better it will disinfect.

WASHING SODA (SODA CRYSTALS OR SODIUM CARBONATE). Cuts grease, removes stains, softens water, and cleans walls, tiles, sinks, and tubs. Be sure to wear compostable rubber gloves to protect your hands when cleaning with it.

NATURAL CLEANING TOOLS

If you were to peek inside my cleaning supplies closet, you'd see a collection of simple, sustainable cleaning tools. I've collected these slowly over the course of several years, sometimes from online shops but, as often as possible, from my local hardware store. Below is a list of tools I either own or covet. You don't need all or even half of them—chosen carefully, a few will go a long way. You may notice that, despite their popularity, microfiber cloths are not on the list—although they do make cleaning easier, unfortunately they introduce microplastics into our water system and pollute streams, rivers, and oceans.

• Cotton string mop with wooden handle (adult and child-size, if needed)

• Wooden Cuban mop and cotton mop cloths, as an alternative to a cotton string mop

• Corn broom with wooden handle (adult and child-size, if needed)

• Split horsehair broom with wooden handle, as an alternative to a corn broom

• Short wooden-handled broom with natural bristles, for cleaning small areas

• Long-handled lamb's wool duster or short-handled goat hair brush, for dusting

• Metal dustpan, for sweeping

• Galvanized steel or enamel buckets, for mopping and washing surfaces

• Small wooden-handled brushes with natural bristles for scrubbing dishes, cleaning fruits and veggies, scouring pots, cleaning bottles, and scrubbing floors

• Wooden-handled toilet brush, stored in a large enamel or metal pitcher

• Copper and/or hemp scrubbers for washing dishes and scrubbing surfaces

• Cotton bar mop towels, flour sack towels, rags cut from old towels and T-shirts, for all manner of cleaning

• Compostable Swedish dish cloths and loofah sponges, for washing dishes

• Glass Parmesan cheese shaker, to store baking soda and make it easy to sprinkle on surfaces

• Glass squirt bottles, for cleaning sprays and air fresheners

• Old bamboo toothbrushes, for cleaning cracks and hard-to-reach places

• Newspapers, for drying windows and glass without leaving streaks

CITRUS ALL-PURPOSE CLEANER

If I were forced to turn in all but one of my homemade cleaning products, this would be the one I'd beg to keep. Citrus-infused all-purpose cleaner is such a simple and pure way to lightly clean your home, and making it is as easy as infusing citrus fruit scraps in a vat of vinegar. It's cheap and easy and eliminates the need for using essential oils to cover up the pungent smell of vinegar. One thing worth noting is that since vinegar is acidic, it can damage certain surfaces and should not be used on natural stones like granite, marble, or soapstone. It can also strip the finish off hardwood floors. Aside from those two surfaces, it can safely clean just about everything else. I use it to clean windows, mirrors, carpets, toilets, tubs, sinks, appliances, and linoleum. **Makes 3 cups vinegar, which can be diluted to make 6 cups citrus cleaner**

INGREDIENTS

2 cups citrus peel strips (lemon, lime, orange, or grapefruit)

3 cups vinegar (apple cider or distilled white), or more as needed

DIRECTIONS

Put the citrus peels in a quart-size glass jar and cover with the vinegar. Cap with a tight-fitting lid or a cloth secured with a rubber band. If using a metal lid, place a piece of compostable parchment paper between the jar and the lid to prevent corrosion. To infuse the vinegar, set the jar in a sunny spot for 2 weeks. Afterward, strain and compost the citrus peels, then pour the infused vinegar into a clean glass jar with an airtight lid.

TO USE In a spray bottle, combine 1 part vinegar and 1 part water, and use as you would any commercial all-purpose cleaner.

TIP If you don't have citrus peels, you can also make an all-purpose cleaner by adding 5 to 10 drops of essential oil to a solution of 1 cup distilled white vinegar and 1 cup water. Green oils like tea tree and eucalyptus work double duty: they have disinfectant qualities and smell wonderful.

GENTLE SURFACE SCRUB

Out of all of my homemade cleaning supplies, I make and use this mild abrasive cleanser the most. I have an old, stain-prone kitchen sink to thank for the hours I've spent experimenting with various commercial and homemade recipes. This recipe uses baking soda as an abrasive, castile soap to remove grease and dirt, hydrogen peroxide to disinfect and brighten, and lemon essential oil to bleach, degrease, deodorize, and disinfect. The scrub can be used on kitchen sinks, countertops, bathroom sinks, tile, grout, and even pots and pans but should not be used on porous surfaces like untreated granite, marble, and wood.

INGREDIENTS

¾ cup baking soda   *1 tablespoon hydrogen peroxide*
¼ cup liquid castile soap   *5 to 10 drops lemon essential oil*

DIRECTIONS

Combine all the ingredients in a medium bowl and stir to form a thick paste. If the paste seems too dry, add more water or hydrogen peroxide. If it seems too wet, add more baking soda. Transfer the paste to an airtight container and store for a few months.

TO USE Place a dab of cleanser on a wooden scrub brush, apply to surface, and scrub. Let the paste sit and work its magic for 10 minutes, then rinse or wipe clean with a damp rag or towel.

HERBAL SCOURING POWDER

If you need something slightly more abrasive than the gentle surface scrub on page 77, this scouring powder should do the trick. You can make it the simple way, with just washing soda, baking soda, and citric acid, or if you're like me and have so many dried herbs you don't know what to do with them, you can add them to the powder to make it more refreshing and abrasive. Any herb with a nice fragrance will do; my favorites are eucalyptus, lavender, lemon balm, peppermint, and rosemary. If you'd like extra bleaching power, a few drops of lemon essential oil will go a long way.

INGREDIENTS

½ cup washing soda, store-bought or homemade (page 100)

½ cup baking soda

2 teaspoons citric acid

½ cup dried herbs (optional)

5 to 10 drops lemon essential oil (optional)

DIRECTIONS

Combine all the ingredients in a medium bowl and then store in an airtight container.

TO USE Sprinkle surface with scouring powder, add water to form a paste, and scrub. Let the paste stand for 10 minutes, then rinse or wipe clean with a damp rag or towel. Be sure to wear gloves, as washing soda is caustic and can irritate the skin.

GRANITE AND MARBLE CLEANER

The trick to maintaining granite and marble countertops is to use the right cleaner. As most manufacturers will tell you, it's important to avoid acidic or harsh cleaners like lemon, ammonia, bleach, or vinegar, as they strip the protective sealant off the stone, making it vulnerable to etching, staining, discoloration, and other damage. Soap and water are often advised, and although that works well for some people, others complain that the soap leaves a film on the surface. Among natural cleaners, alcohol works well on stone—it's pH neutral, evaporates quickly, and has the added bonus of being a disinfectant. If you like the refreshing scent of citrus cleaners, you can also add lemon or citrus essential oils. Although they're derived from citrus fruits, essential oils are pH neutral and safe to use for cleaning stone.

INGREDIENTS

¼ cup high-proof vodka (80 to 100 percent) or rubbing alcohol

1½ cups water

½ teaspoon liquid castile soap

10 drops lemon essential oil (optional)

DIRECTIONS

Combine all the ingredients in a large mixing bowl and mix thoroughly. Using a funnel, pour the mixture into a 16-ounce glass spray bottle and cap tightly.

PRE-VACUUM RUG CLEANER

This simple cleaner is a great way to freshen and deodorize rugs and carpets without artificial fragrances. I vacuum several times a week, but I give rugs a spiffing-up with this cleaner about once a month.

INGREDIENTS

1 cup dried lavender flowers (optional)

2 cups baking soda

10 drops lavender essential oil

10 drops rose geranium essential oil

DIRECTIONS

If using the lavender flowers, crush them into a medium bowl, then mix in the baking soda. Add the essential oils and blend well. Transfer the mixture to a glass jar with an airtight lid.

TO USE Sprinkle on rugs or carpets, let sit for 30 minutes, then vacuum as usual.

HARDWOOD FLOOR CLEANER

I don't clean the floors nearly as often as I should, but when I do, I like to do it the old-fashioned way—on my hands and knees and with very few ingredients. I use castile soap instead of vinegar, which is believed by some to be too acidic for, and potentially damaging to, hardwood floors. This recipe has worked wonderfully for me for years, and I love that you can add essential oils to disinfect and deodorize the house. My favorite oils for cleaning floors are tea tree, eucalyptus, lavender, lemon, and peppermint.

INGREDIENTS

2 cups warm water   *5 to 10 drops essential oil (optional)*

2 drops castile soap or Sal Suds

DIRECTIONS

In a large bowl, mix all the ingredients. Pour into a 16-ounce glass spray bottle, seal tightly, and shake well.

TO USE Spray on floors and either mop up with a cotton string mop or wooden Cuban mop or get on your hands and knees and wipe up the solution with a bar mop towel.

OVEN CLEANER

Commercial oven cleaners are among the most toxic household cleaning products. The Environmental Working Group (EWG) recommends avoiding them altogether. Not only do they contain powerful corrosive agents like sodium hydroxide, which can severely burn the skin and damage the eyes, but their grease-dissolving ingredients irritate the eyes, skin, and mucous membranes. Did I mention EWG also says they can damage the kidneys, lungs, and neurological system? Needless to say, this is one cleaning product I would never invite into my home, much less into the kitchen where we eat!

Fortunately, there's a simple and effective way to clean the oven without using harsh cleaners. Just create a paste with baking soda and water, put on a pair of gloves, and use your hands to spread it inside the oven (away from the heating elements). Leave the paste overnight, then use a damp cloth to wipe it clean in the morning. If that doesn't work and you need something slightly more powerful, the following recipe will do the trick. It requires some mechanical cleaning, or what our grandmothers might call elbow grease, but it works well on even the grimiest of ovens.

INGREDIENTS

5 tablespoons baking soda

5 tablespoons washing soda, store-bought or homemade (page 100)

2 tablespoons liquid castile soap

Warm water, as needed

Distilled white vinegar, in a spray bottle

DIRECTIONS

Make sure the oven is off and completely cool. Remove all racks and removable parts. Give the oven and door a good wipe-down to remove food debris. In a small bowl, mix the baking soda, washing soda, and castile soap. Add just enough warm water to form a foamy paste. Using a glove, scoop out the paste, one handful at a time, and spread it all over the door and interior surfaces of the oven, away from the heating elements. Close the door and let the paste sit for a few hours or overnight. With a wooden scrub brush or copper scrub pad, scrub any areas coated in a heavy residue. Finally, spray all surfaces with vinegar and wipe clean.

LEMON LIQUID DISH SOAP

When it comes to hand-washing dishes, I like to use a wooden-handled scrub brush and a bar of savon de Marseilles. A traditional olive oil–based soap, savon de Marseilles has been around for six hundred years and makes an excellent alternative to chemical and petroleum-based soaps. Culturally, we're in the habit of using liquid soaps for dishwashing, but bar soaps work just as well in terms of cleaning. That said, if you really love your liquid soaps, which I do understand, here is one recipe that is simple and sudsy—perhaps not quite like a big dollop of Palmolive, but definitely more so than plain castile soap.

INGREDIENTS

½ cup water (preferably distilled)   *1 tablespoon jojoba or almond oil*

2 tablespoons distilled white vinegar   *1 tablespoon vitamin E oil (optional)*

½ cup Sal Suds   *10 drops lemon essential oil (optional)*

DIRECTIONS

Using a small funnel, pour the water and vinegar into a glass soap pump dispenser. Cap and shake well. Add the Sal Suds, jojoba oil, and vitamin E oil and lemon oil, if using.

TO USE Tip the bottle upside down and right side up a few times to gently mix ingredients before using.

VEGGIE WASHES

Try as I might to buy organic fruits and veggies, sometimes there's no avoiding produce that's been treated with pesticides. Even when I do buy organic, there's still bacteria, dirt, and grime to consider. In the United States there's even something called diphenylamine (DPA), which is applied to apples to keep them fresh for longer periods of time. Commercial veggie washes purport to remove pesticides, wax, dirt, and other residues. While these sprays are generally made from plant-based sources and appear to be safe, the question is whether they're actually worth the money—and plastic waste.

A few years ago when I looked into making my own veggie wash, I discovered a study by *Cooks Illustrated* showing that diluted vinegar was effective at removing 98 percent of bacteria. The same study found that a scrub brush removed 85 percent of bacteria. A separate study published by *Consumer Reports* found that soaking apples in a baking soda solution completely removed three pesticides being tested. Having found these and other studies, I started making my own cleaning solutions, including a baking soda soak, a vinegar soak, and a vinegar spray. I don't think one of these solutions is necessarily better than the others, but I like having options in case I'm short an ingredient or am washing different types of produce. The vinegar spray works best on smooth-skinned fruits and veggies, such as apples, pears, cucumbers, and peppers, while the vinegar and baking soda soaks work well for delicate produce like berries and mushrooms. For produce with thick skin, I also use a vegetable brush to help wash away hard-to-remove residue.

VINEGAR SPRAY. Fill a spray bottle with 1 part distilled white vinegar and 3 parts warm water. Spray the produce, give it a quick scrub, and rinse clean with tap water.

VINEGAR SOAK. Fill a large bowl with 1 part vinegar and 3 parts warm water. Mix well, add the produce, and allow it to soak for 15 minutes. If possible, scrub the produce with a veggie brush and then rinse clean with water.

BAKING SODA SOAK. Fill a large bowl with 2 quarts warm water. Add 2 tablespoons baking soda and mix well. Add the produce and allow it to soak for 10 to 15 minutes. If possible, scrub the produce with a veggie brush and then rinse clean with water.

DISHWASHER DETERGENT

Dishwasher detergent is the holy grail of DIY home cleaning. The first few recipes I tried were disappointing, to say the least. They left my dishes spotty and streaked and made me wonder if they looked cleaner going into the dishwasher than coming out. After much research and trial and error, I came up with two ways to win at washing dishes the nontoxic, low-waste way—by using a dishwasher powder (this page) and by making your own dishwasher tabs (page 92).

INGREDIENTS

1 tablespoon washing soda, store-bought or homemade (page 100)

¼ teaspoon citric acid

2 tablespoons distilled white vinegar

DIRECTIONS

Note that you can't combine the dry ingredients ahead of time—they'll clump together like cement and make it difficult to scoop out of the container. You'll need to store the washing soda in one container and the citric acid in another one. When you're ready to do a load of dishes, add the washing soda and citric acid, separately, to the wash compartment of the dishwasher. Add the vinegar to the rinse compartment. Close the compartment doors, run the dishwasher, and wait for the surprise of your life!

Dishwasher Detergent Tabs (page 92)

DISHWASHER DETERGENT TABS

If you're accustomed to using dishwasher tabs but want to avoid single-use packaging, this homemade version is wonderful. However, they'll leave your dishes spotty without the addition of vinegar, so be sure to include the last step where you add it to the rinse compartment. You'll need a silicone mold like the ones commonly used for candy-making; just be sure the size of the finished tabs will fit inside your dishwasher.

INGREDIENTS

1 cup washing soda, store-bought or homemade (page 100)

1 cup baking soda

¼ cup citric acid

1 cup kosher salt

5 drops essential oil (optional)

1 cup water

Distilled white vinegar, as needed

DIRECTIONS

Combine the washing soda, baking soda, citric acid, salt, and essential oil, if using, in a bowl and mix well. Add the water slowly to try to prevent too much of a reaction. Mix the ingredients slowly but thoroughly, then spoon the mixture into silicone molds. Allow the mixture to dry and harden for about an hour. Once hardened, remove the tabs from the mold and store them in an airtight container.

TO USE Use one tab per load, along with 2 tablespoons of distilled white vinegar added to the rinse compartment.

NATURAL DRAIN CLEANER

You know what all old farmhouses have in common? Old plumbing! The first time I tried making my own toothpaste with coconut oil, I learned just how unforgiving old pipes can be. Not wanting to pay a plumber, and having only simple ingredients on hand, I used this "natural Drano." Much to my surprise (and relief!), it worked. Although in natural cleaning, you don't usually mix baking soda and vinegar (they neutralize one another, rendering each ineffective), the chemical reaction that takes place between them does a fine job at unclogging pipes.

INGREDIENTS

1 cup baking soda *1 cup distilled white vinegar*

1 cup table salt *Boiling water*

DIRECTIONS

To unclog a sink or tub, simply sprinkle the baking soda down the drain, followed by the table salt and distilled white vinegar. The mixture will foam and bubble, just like the volcanoes you used to make in elementary school. Wait 5 to 10 minutes to let them work their magic, then flush the solution down with a pot of boiling water.

TOILET PODS

Although I love the idea of doing a deep clean once a week, there are some areas of the house that can't wait that long. With traffic from children, a husband, friends, and extended family, our bathrooms need light cleaning two or three times a week. For convenience, I keep a tray of cleaning supplies in the bathroom cupboards that makes it easy to do a quick clean. Our bathroom trays hold a scrub brush, a cleaning rag, all-purpose cleaner (page 74), gentle surface scrub (page 77), and a jar of these toilet-cleaning pods. I use one every couple of days for maintenance and follow up with a deep clean once a week using the cleaner on page 97.

INGREDIENTS

1 cup baking soda   *1 tablespoon hydrogen peroxide*

¼ cup citric acid   *15 drops essential oil (optional)*

1 tablespoon Sal Suds

DIRECTIONS

Combine the baking soda and citric acid in a medium bowl and mix well. Slowly add the Sal Suds, hydrogen peroxide, and essential oil (if using). Take your time to prevent activating the dry ingredients. Stir until the mixture has the consistency of wet sand. Pack the mixture into silicone candy molds and allow to dry for a few hours. Once dry, transfer the pods to an airtight container and store until ready to use.

TO USE Drop one pod in the toilet, wait for it to stop fizzing, then scrub the toilet with a wooden brush.

TOILET BOWL CLEANER

In general, there are three ways to clean—chemically, mechanically, or thermally. When you choose to avoid harsh chemicals, sometimes you have to make up for it mechanically, by using a little muscle. While the toilet pods from the previous recipe (page 94) will help keep toilet bowls "clean enough" throughout the week, I like to use this recipe once a week to give toilets a deep clean.

INGREDIENTS

2 cups distilled water

1⅓ cups baking soda

⅓ cup liquid castile soap

20 drops eucalyptus, lemon, or tea tree essential oil

Hydrogen peroxide

DIRECTIONS

Combine the water, baking soda, and soap in a large bowl and mix thoroughly. Using a funnel, transfer the mixture to an empty squeeze bottle. Add the essential oils, cap, and shake well.

TO USE Turn off the toilet water by turning the knob on the wall under the toilet clockwise all the way. Flush the toilet once or twice to drain the water from the bowl. Squirt the solution under the rim of the bowl and allow to sit for 5 minutes. Scrub with a toilet brush, turn the water back on, and flush. To disinfect the toilet, fill a spray bottle with hydrogen peroxide, spritz the toilet bowl, and swish with the brush.

LAUNDRY SOAP

This homemade laundry soap is simple, inexpensive, and made up of ingredients that score the highest safety rating by the Environmental Working Group. The castile soap cleans clothes, cuts grease, and removes stains; the washing soda softens water, removes stains, and whitens clothes; the baking soda removes stains, eliminates odors, and whitens and softens clothes; and the salt acts as a fabric softener. Because it's naturally low-sudsing, this soap can be used in both standard and high-efficiency machines. It's worth mentioning that this is laundry soap—not detergent. (Chemically, soaps aren't as strong as detergents; laundry detergent in particular is often chemically formulated for washing machines.) If you find that your clothes aren't getting as clean as you'd like, you can add 2 or 3 tablespoons of Dr. Bronner's Sal Suds to each load of laundry. As a natural surfactant and detergent, Sal Suds is particularly effective at treating stains and odors.

INGREDIENTS

One 5-ounce bar pure castile soap

1 cup washing soda, store-bought or homemade (page 100)

1 cup baking soda

1 cup coarse salt

DIRECTIONS

Chop the soap into small cubes, put them in the bowl of a food processor, and blitz until finely ground. (If you don't own a food processor, you can also use a hand grater—it'll take a little longer but works just fine.) Add the washing soda, baking soda, and salt to the food processor and blend into a fine powder. Store in a glass container with an airtight lid.

TO USE Use 2 tablespoons per load for standard machines and 1 tablespoon per load for high-efficiency machines.

HOMEMADE WASHING SODA

Several recipes in this book call for washing soda, which you should be able to find in most grocery stores. If you can't find it locally and you don't want to buy it online, you can also make it yourself by heating baking soda in the oven. When it comes to cleaning, baking soda (sodium bicarbonate) and washing soda (sodium carbonate) are quite different, but chemically the only difference between the two is the presence of water and carbon dioxide. On a practical level, that means that when you heat baking soda, it breaks down into water steam, carbon dioxide, and washing soda; the steam and carbon dioxide dissipate, leaving the washing soda behind.

Baking soda is mild, with a pH of 8, while washing soda is caustic, with a pH of 11. Washing soda's high alkalinity allows it to act as a solvent in removing stains. But it also makes it harsh on the skin, so you should always wear gloves when handling it.

INGREDIENTS

2 to 3 cups baking soda

DIRECTIONS

1. Preheat the oven to 400°F.

2. Sprinkle the baking soda evenly on a rimmed baking sheet and bake for 30 minutes to 1 hour, stirring occasionally so that it bakes evenly. You'll know the baking soda has been converted to washing soda when the consistency and color change: Whereas baking soda has a fine, powdery texture and white color, washing soda is coarse, with a slight yellow tint.

3. Let cool and store in an airtight jar. Add to homemade cleaning solutions as directed in the recipes.

FABRIC SOFTENER

Fabric softeners sound good in theory—they reduce wrinkles and static cling, prevent stretching, fading, and pilling, and leave clothes feeling softer and smelling fresh. But are they worth it? The Environmental Working Group recommends avoiding commercial fabric softeners because they contain chemicals that trigger asthma and damage the reproductive system. They're also believed to harm the environment and cause indoor and outdoor air pollution. As an alternative, you can add vinegar to the rinse cycle to smooth natural fibers and reduce static cling. If you're concerned about the smell of vinegar, don't worry—it dissipates when the clothing dries.

INGREDIENTS

1 quart distilled white vinegar   *10 drops essential oil (optional)*

DIRECTIONS

Combine the vinegar with the essential oil (if using) and store in an airtight quart-size glass jar.

TO USE When ready to wash clothes, add ½ cup to the rinse cycle compartment or to the main compartment when the rinse cycle begins.

REUSABLE DRYER SHEETS

I mostly line-dry our clothes, but I know plenty of eco-conscious people who still use dryers. If you fall into that group and love dryer sheets for softening fabrics, reducing static, and adding fragrance, here's a recipe that will do all of that without creating waste or exposing you to artificial fragrances and harmful toxins.

MATERIALS

100% cotton rags, T-shirts, or washcloths

2½ cups water

2½ cups distilled white vinegar

3 tablespoons vegetable glycerin

10 drops essential oils (optional)

DIRECTIONS

Cut old cotton rags, T-shirts, and/or washcloths into 5-by-8-inch rectangles (about 20 is a good quantity for a quart-size jar). If necessary, stitch around the edges to prevent unraveling. Combine the water, vinegar, and glycerin in a quart-size jar. Close the lid and shake vigorously. Add the essential oils and shake again. Place the rags in the jar and seal it until you're ready to use them.

TO USE Remove 2 to 4 dryer sheets from the jar, wring them so they're not dripping, and add them to the dryer load. When the cloths are dry, simply put the sheets back in the jar and use them again. Launder with towels and linens once every 2 weeks, depending on usage.

HOMEMADE WOOL DRYER BALLS

Wool dryer balls are an eco-friendly alternative to fabric softeners and dryer sheets. Not only do they soften your clothes, but they also eliminate static, decrease wrinkling, and reduce drying time by up to 25 percent. They're free of synthetic fragrances, too, although you can certainly add a fresh scent to your clothes by using essential oils. You'll want to do this at the end of the drying cycle, however, since heat will destroy the essential oils. Once your clothes are dry, simply add a few drops to the dryer balls, return the balls to the dryer, and run on cold ("air-dry") for a few minutes.

MATERIALS

1 skein 100% wool roving yarn (not machine-washable yarn, which won't felt)

Scissors

Felting needle or crochet hook

1 pair old or thrifted pantyhose or stockings

Laundry soap, store-bought or homemade (page 98)

DIRECTIONS

1. Start your first wool dryer ball by wrapping the yarn around your index and middle fingers 10 to 15 times. Remove the yarn from your fingers and twist in the shape of a figure 8 to form a bundle. Wrap more yarn around the center of the bundle 10 to 15 times. Continue wrapping, alternating directions, until the bundle starts to look like a small ball. Keep wrapping until it's the size of a large tennis ball. Cut the yarn from the skein. Using a felting needle or crochet hook, tuck the tail of the yarn under several layers of the ball. This should keep the ball from unraveling during the felting process. Make 5 more balls.

2. Cut off the legs of the pantyhose and stuff 3 balls in each leg. Separate the balls by tying a piece of yarn between each ball, then tie off the top of the pantyhose. Place the hose in the washing machine, add detergent, and wash on high heat. Dry on high heat until the balls are dry and felted (the yarn strands have fused together). Remove the balls from the pantyhose.

TO USE Toss 3 dryer balls into the dryer, add clean, wet laundry, and dry as usual. If you experience static problems, try drying your clothes for a shorter amount of time. You can also try spritzing your dryer balls with water before tossing them in with laundry. The water will combine with the heat in the dryer to create steam, which will reduce static.

TIPS FOR LINE-DRYING

Line-drying is a simple task from a slower time, and although it may seem like a relic of the past, there are lots of reasons to include it in a modern-day laundry routine. While it conserves energy and saves you money, it also extends the life of your clothes and linens. If germs and stains are a concern, you'll appreciate that the sun is a powerful disinfectant with natural bleaching power. I'd also argue that line-drying is therapeutic. Being outside in the warm sunshine, working methodically with your hands—I can't think of a better way to slow down and be present. Here are a few tips to help you get started.

• Choose a rot-resistant clothesline, set it up in an area that gets a nice breeze and plenty of sunshine, and make sure it's taut, well anchored, and within reach but also high enough to keep laundry off the ground.

• To avoid wrinkled clothes, give them a shake and snap before hanging them and a good tug once pinned to the line.

• To further avoid stiffness and wrinkling, use a natural fabric softener during the rinse cycle (see page 101), fold clothes as soon as you take them off the line, and/or give clothes a quick 5-minute spin in the dryer after line-drying just to soften them.

• To brighten whites, hang them at the front of the line, in direct sunlight. To reduce fading, turn bright or dark clothes inside out and hang them toward the back of the line or in the shade.

• To prevent bunching or clothespin marks, hang casual shirts upside down from the bottom seam, dress shirts on a hanger, and pants and skirts from the waistband.

• Avoid hanging stretchy knits that can lose their shape; instead, lay them flat on an elevated drying screen.

• To promote good circulation, leave space between clothes and linens; hang towels from the shorter end; and fold sheets in half and clip the corners of the open ends to the clothesline.

• For small items like socks and underwear that take up a lot of space on the line, either double them up and overlap pins or hang them on a portable wooden drying rack.

• To keep your line taut, hang heavy items at the ends of your clothesline and lighter items in the middle.

• When you're all done, be sure to bring your clothespins indoors to prevent wear and tear.

• If you don't have an outdoor area, line-dry indoors instead. You can either set up a retractable clothesline in the shower or hang clothes on curtain rods, drawer knobs, radiators, or drying racks.

STAIN REMOVERS

Commercial stain removal products are some of the most toxic cleaners available. They often contain harsh chemicals, solvents, parabens, sulfates, artificial colors, and fragrances. You can avoid exposure by trying one or all of the following home-made removers. I like having multiple recipes to turn to in case I run out of an ingredient. As with most spot removers, these work best if you treat stains immediately and allow the fabric to soak before throwing it in the washing machine. Treating stains on the opposite side of the fabric helps avoid making them worse.

STAIN REMOVER RECIPE 1

Combine the following ingredients in a glass spray bottle, mix well, apply to stains, and allow to set for an hour before adding the clothes to the wash.

¾ cup water

2 tablespoons liquid castile soap

2 tablespoons vegetable glycerin

5 drops lemon essential oil

STAIN REMOVER RECIPE 2

Combine the following ingredients in an amber glass spray bottle (to prevent the hydrogen peroxide from oxidizing), mix well, use to pretreat spots, and allow to set for an hour before adding the clothes to the wash.

¼ cup hydrogen peroxide

2 tablespoons liquid castile soap

20 drops lemon essential oil

STAIN REMOVER RECIPE 3

Combine the following ingredients in an amber glass spray bottle (to prevent the hydrogen peroxide from oxidizing), mix well, apply to stains, and allow to set for an hour before adding the clothes to the wash.

¼ cup water

¼ cup liquid castile soap

¼ cup vegetable glycerin

1 tablespoon hydrogen peroxide

20 drops lemon essential oil

continued

LAUNDRY BOOSTER

After spot cleaning with one of the recipes on page 108, you can use this laundry booster to help clean and brighten soiled clothes. Just add the following quantities of each ingredient to a load. The booster should be used with laundry soap or detergent as it helps them perform better.

½ cup hydrogen peroxide

½ cup washing soda

BLEACH ALTERNATIVE

To naturally brighten whites, add this mixture to the wash. The sun also works well to brighten whites—if you have a clothesline, be sure to dry your clothes outside!

¾ cup hydrogen peroxide

20 drops lemon essential oil

WINDOW AND GLASS CLEANER

I grew up in the South and went to college in historical Charleston, South Carolina. I'm not sure there's anything I love more than a really old home, with a front porch, big windows, and oodles of natural light. Our current home is an old farmhouse with lots of big windows and a lot of natural light that is often obstructed by fingerprints, window drawings, and puppy lick marks. What can I say—we have two children and a very excitable puppy! The bathroom mirrors don't stay clean for long either. Needless to say, I've had plenty of experience with homemade window and glass cleaners and can vouch for what does and doesn't work. If you try to use vinegar and paper towels, for example, there's a good chance you'll walk away thinking your windows looked better before you tried to clean them!

Instead, for light cleaning, use a solution of 1 part distilled white vinegar to 1 part water, along with a terrycloth towel or newspaper to wipe away streaks. You'll want to avoid paper towels and old rags as they tend to leave behind lint and dust.

For heavy-duty cleaning, I use the following recipe. It contains cornstarch, which is a magical ingredient for streak-free, sparkly glass and windows.

INGREDIENTS

2 tablespoons rubbing alcohol or vodka

2 tablespoons distilled white vinegar

1 tablespoon cornstarch

1½ cups warm water

3 to 5 drops essential oil (optional)

DIRECTIONS

Combine all the ingredients in a 16-ounce glass spray bottle, cap, and shake well. Spray on windows and wipe clean with newspaper or terrycloth.

TIP Be sure to shake well before using, as the cornstarch will settle to the bottom between uses.

WOOD BUTTER

As I like to say, "Love your things, and they'll love you back." When it comes to wood, nothing could be closer to the truth. Before I knew better, I used to toss wooden spoons and cutting boards in the dishwasher and then wonder why they cracked so easily. I learned the hard way that they last a lifetime only when they're well cared for. Nowadays, to prevent mold and moisture, I hand-wash them in warm water with mild soap and dry them immediately with a dish towel. For deep cleaning, I rinse them in distilled white vinegar or lemon juice. And to prevent cracking and splitting, I condition them with this simple, natural, low-waste wood butter.

INGREDIENTS AND MATERIALS

2 tablespoons beeswax   *Wooden popsicle stick*

6 tablespoons unrefined coconut oil

DIRECTIONS

Pour 2 inches of water into the bottom of a double boiler (see page 127 for how to make your own double boiler) and bring to a simmer over medium heat. Combine the beeswax and coconut oil in the top of the double boiler and heat until they melt. Stir with the popsicle stick, then pour the mixture into a glass jar. Let the mixture set at room temperature, then cap the jar with an airtight lid and store the wood butter in a cool, dark place.

TO USE To condition wooden utensils and cutting boards, make sure they are clean and dry, then apply a thin layer of wood butter to the surface, buff with a clean, soft cloth, and allow to soak up the oils overnight.

NATURAL
WELLNESS

Long before modern medicine came along, people treated all manner of ailments with simple homemade remedies. They grew herbs in their gardens, foraged plants from wild places, and occasionally purchased dried herbs, tinctures, and salves from local pharmacies and apothecaries. They cooked nutrient-rich soups, made poultices for wounds, and prepared syrups for cold and flu season. Traditional healing was the people's medicine, and it was usually practiced in the comfort of one's home.

Growing up, I remember my grandparents didn't so much as sniff when it came to treating minor injuries and illnesses. If my grandmother burned her finger on the stove, she would break off a piece of aloe and spread the gel on her wound. If a grandchild was stung by a bee, my grandfather would make a poultice out of plantain from his backyard. When I lived in Guinea, my host father, a shaman, made all sorts of medicines from plants surrounding our village.

In my own life, especially since becoming a mother, I've had lots of opportunities to use natural wellness remedies. While I don't believe that natural wellness should replace conventional medicine in all cases, for minor ailments I've found it to be a simple and empowering way to enhance my family's well-being. Thankfully, I've had the support of some wonderful health practitioners, including our pediatrician, who was trained in both conventional and homeopathic medicine. I give her full credit for introducing me to simple, gentle approaches to healing. When I had mastitis, she taught me to make a poultice out of cabbage leaves. For my kids' ear infections, she showed me how to use onions to draw out inflammation and fight infection. She gave us recipes for soups and teas to help fight a cold or flu, and when my daughter was teething, she taught me how to use clove oil to ease the pain.

Here is how I stock our wellness cabinet, along with a handful of simple remedies I use on myself and my family. As you peruse this section, keep in mind that I'm not a health practitioner and am simply sharing remedies that have worked for me. You should talk with your doctor before attempting to treat yourself or someone else.

NATURAL WELLNESS ESSENTIALS

Making home remedies isn't difficult. Often it's a matter of cooking up a pot of soup, infusing a cup of tea, diffusing some essential oils, or making a salve from herbs you've grown in your garden. For me, the secret to treating minor ailments has been in keeping a moderately well-stocked wellness cabinet. I started small with a book of herbal remedies by Rosemary Gladstar, some chamomile tea, and a jar of arnica salve. My collection grew slowly, sometimes one ingredient at a time, as I learned new recipes. Below is a list of the essential ingredients, equipment, essential oils, and herbs I stock for the remedies and recipes in this book.

BASIC INGREDIENTS

- Alcohol (80-proof: brandy, gin, or vodka)
- Apple cider vinegar, store-bought or homemade (page 34)
- Arrowroot powder
- Baking soda
- Beeswax
- Candelilla wax (vegan)
- Clay, bentonite or French
- Cocoa butter
- Coconut oil
- Cold-pressed organic olive oil
- Epsom salts
- Fractionated coconut oil
- Grass-fed gelatin
- Jojoba oil
- Liquid castile soap
- Oatmeal
- Pine resin
- Raw honey
- Rosehip seed oil
- Shea butter
- Sweet almond oil
- Vegetable glycerin
- Vitamin E oil
- Witch hazel extract
- Xylitol

EQUIPMENT

- Blender or food processor
- Candy thermometer
- Containers (jars, tins, lip balm tubes, roll-on bottles)
- Double boiler (see page 127)
- Funnels
- Infusers for loose leaf tea
- Kitchen scale
- Labels for jars
- Measuring cups and spoons
- Pipettes and/or eyedroppers
- Silicone molds
- Strainer
- Teakettle or saucepan
- Teapot
- Wooden popsicle sticks

ESSENTIAL OILS

- Bergamot
- Cedarwood
- Citronella
- Eucalyptus
- Frankincense
- Geranium
- Helichrysum
- Lavender
- Lemon
- Lemongrass
- Patchouli
- Peppermint
- Rosemary
- Tea tree
- Vetiver

HERBS AND SPICES

- Aloe vera
- Arnica
- Burdock root
- Calendula flowers
- Catnip
- Chamomile flowers
- Cinnamon
- Cloves
- Comfrey
- Dandelion
- Echinacea root and flowers
- Elderberry
- Feverfew
- Garlic
- Ginger
- Hops
- Hyssop
- Lavender
- Lemon balm
- Licorice root
- Marshmallow
- Nettles
- Oatstraw
- Passionflower
- Peppermint
- Plantain
- Rose petals
- Sage
- Skullcap
- Thyme
- Turmeric

GATHERING AND SOURCING HERBS

After looking at the lists of natural wellness essentials on pages 117 and 118, you may feel the urge to start gathering and sourcing as many herbs as possible. Rest assured, a simple collection of five to ten herbs is plenty, especially since a smaller collection will allow you to really get to know each herb, including its many uses and versatility.

If you garden, you can grow most herbs in your backyard. Some can be wild-foraged, others purchased locally at food cooperatives or natural grocery stores. If you have access to a farmers' market, you may be able to buy them fresh or dried from local growers. Otherwise, I recommend procuring dried herbs from a trusted online company that supports fair trade and sustainable practices (see page 124).

If you choose to forage herbs, you'll want to do it safely and sustainably. Harvest only what you can identify with confidence, either with the help of a guidebook or a seasoned forager. Avoid plants growing near roads, railroads, old homes, and powerlines, as the surrounding soil can be contaminated with lead, herbicides, and other toxins. Fields that have been sprayed with herbicides and floodplains near polluted rivers should be off-limits as well.

When it comes to sustainability, remember to harvest plants that are abundant and plentiful, avoid foraging rare or less populous species, and focus on nonnative over native species. Make sure you're harvesting responsibly by ensuring that it's legal to gather plants in a particular area.

DRYING AND STORING HERBS

If you grow or gather herbs yourself, you can follow the instructions for drying them on page 219. I use dried herbs for many of the recipes in this book, mostly because they can be stored and accessed year-round but also because products made with dried herbs are less likely to spoil. I recommend storing loose, dried herbs in glass jars with tight-fitting lids.

When it comes to setting up your wellness cabinet, I recommend finding a spot in your kitchen, where you're likely to prepare remedies. Since herbs are best kept away from heat and sunlight, the ideal location is in a cabinet away from the oven and stove. Some people keep their herbs on a bookshelf, covered with a fabric sheet, which works just fine, too.

Keep track of when you harvested, dried, purchased, or prepared your herbs by clearly labeling and dating your jars and containers. Most dried herbs maintain their potency and vibrancy for 1 to 2 years. To prevent waste, harvest or purchase only as much as you plan to use in the upcoming year.

ESSENTIAL OILS

Aside from herbs, your wellness cabinet will likely be stocked with a handful of useful and versatile essential oils. Essential oils are the volatile liquids distilled from plants and are often called the "life force" or "soul" of the plant. They're highly concentrated and must be used with caution. To put their potency in perspective, one drop of essential oil is the equivalent of 15 to 40 cups of medicinal tea or 10 teaspoons of a tincture. For this reason, it's important to educate yourself on the properties and potential contraindications of essential oils before using them. For safety, most essential oils should be diluted in a carrier oil, such as fractionated coconut oil, jojoba oil, or sweet almond oil, rather than applied directly to the skin. Remember that diluting essential oils doesn't make them weak—it makes them safe!

Before using an essential oil, I recommend doing a patch test to rule out sensitivities. Simply combine a drop or two of the essential oil in question with ½ teaspoon of a carrier oil, mix the ingredients well, dab them with a small piece of cloth, and tape the cloth to the inside of your wrist. Leave the cloth on your skin for 12 to 24 hours. If the area becomes irritated or red, you'll want to avoid using that particular oil in in any of your remedies.

ESSENTIAL OIL QUALITY AND SUSTAINABILITY

When it comes to sourcing essential oils, it's important to consider quality *and* sustainability. The last few decades have seen a resurgence in the use of essential oils, thanks in large part to a growing interest in natural cleaning and wellness. The problem is that greater demand has resulted in increased supply, making it difficult for consumers to discern whether they're buying pure, safe, high-quality oils. It doesn't help that there are no government regulations or certifications to classify oils according to quality.

Another factor to consider is sustainability. It would be remiss to write a book about living simply and sustainably without discussing the potential environmental impacts of essential oils. As much as I love using them for cleaning and wellness, I do worry about the impacts mass distribution has on the lands and communities that produce them. Because they are a concentrated product, it takes an extraordinary amount of plant material to produce a small amount of an essential oil: One pound of essential oil requires, for example, 10,000 pounds of rose petals, 2,000 pounds of cypress, 6,000 pounds of lemon balm, 250 pounds of lavender buds, or 1,500 lemons. That's a lot of natural resources, and the impacts can be devasting depending on how and at what scale the plants are grown and harvested.

Many large-scale distributers work with corporate farms that use a farming practice known as monocropping, which often leads to depleted soils, biodiversity loss, and the use of pesticides and herbicides. Seeking out essential oils that bear organic certification is the easiest way to guarantee that they were grown without synthetic fertilizers, pesticides, herbicides, irradiation, or genetic engineering. However, some companies forego organic certification since the system isn't specific to essential oils. You can contact a company to learn more about their sustainability policies and sourcing methods.

Wild-harvesting is one alternative to large-scale farming. Because the plants are harvested from the wild, they're unlikely to be contaminated with pesticides. However, this practice can lead to overharvesting—a few popular essential oils come from plants that are endangered or threatened. Fortunately, there are companies committed to producing oils that are organic, herbicide-free, and ethically wild-harvested. Mountain Rose Herbs, for example, sells oils that are certified organic and that are wild-harvested according to ethical harvesting guidelines.

Aside from concerns over how essential oils are produced, there's also the issue of disposal. Each essential oil should have a material safety data sheet (MSDS) that provides toxicity information, flammability warnings, and disposal directions. You can usually find this information on the distributor's website. Many oils, like tea tree, frankincense, and eucalyptus, are flammable and require extra precautions when disposing of them. Some of the oils are considered hazardous waste, which means their containers can't be recycled unless properly cleaned and washed. Even then, some municipalities require that any glass containers that previously held flammable or hazardous materials be thrown in the trash. Some companies, like Rocky Mountain Oils, offer recycling programs that accept bottles back and will recycle them for you. I hope other large distributors will take responsibility and follow their lead.

Despite these concerns, essential oils make wonderful alternatives to toxic chemicals used in cleaning and are a powerful tool for natural wellness. Instead of abandoning them completely, perhaps we should focus on using them mindfully and at least *more* sustainably. One page 124 I offer a few tips that have helped me vet companies on the grounds of quality and sustainability. While you may not be able to find one company that meets all of these guidelines, you'll at least have a way to think critically so you can make a prudent decision.

QUALITY AND SAFETY

• Consider the cost of the essential oils. A high-quality oil should feel like an investment, whereas an inexpensive bottle might be a sign that the oils have been diluted with cheap ingredients.

• Read the ingredients list and make sure diluents such as almond oil or grapeseed oil are not included.

• Look for certified organic, unsprayed, or wildcrafted essential oils, as chemical pollutants can be highly concentrated in essential oils.

• Make sure the company uses gas chromatography–mass spectrometry (GC-MS) to test and validate the quality of every batch of oil they receive. Responsible vendors will either make these reports available on their websites or provide them upon request.

• Try to source essential oils that are labeled with the plant's scientific or botanical name, the country of origin, and the distillation date.

• Purchase essential oils that have been packaged in dark glass bottles that protect them from light.

ETHICS AND SUSTAINABILITY

• Do your research and support companies that use ethical and sustainable practices. Some companies are members of the National Association for Holistic Aromatherapy and must abide by NAHA's ethics standards. You can find a list of NAHA members on its website.

• Become familiar with endangered or threatened plants and substitute essential oils made from plants that are abundant and plentiful.

• Use oils responsibly and sparingly. Dilute them instead of using them directly on your skin, use them purposefully and when you truly need them, and avoid using them frivolously—for example, by diffusing them to make the house smell good.

• Commit to properly disposing of and recycling essential oil bottles. Find a company that accepts bottles for recycling. If that service isn't available, dispose of oils following the recommendations of your local waste management company.

STORING ESSENTIAL OILS

Essential oils retain their healing properties for 5 to 10 years if properly stored in a cool, dark place. The exception to this is citrus oils, which retain their potency for only 6 to 12 months, unless stored in the refrigerator, where they're likely to last for a couple of years. To prolong the shelf life of your oils, use a screw-on cap instead of a rubber dropper top. With the latter, the strong vapors will gradually deteriorate the rubber and allow air to enter the bottle, causing the precious volatile properties to evaporate prematurely.

SAFETY CONSIDERATIONS

Although the remedies in this book are generally safe to use, there are a few considerations that should be noted.

• The remedies in this book are meant to treat mild symptoms. Always seek professional medical advice and care if symptoms are serious.

• Dried herbs, herbal preparations, and essential oils should be kept safely out of reach of children and pets.

• Check with a pediatrician before administering essential oils or herbal preparations to children.

• Pregnant or breastfeeding women should always consult a health practitioner before using essential oils or herbal remedies.

• Individuals with serious medical conditions or autoimmune disorders should consult a health practitioner before using essential oils or herbal remedies.

• Individuals taking medication should consult with a healthcare practitioner to check for contraindications before using a home remedy.

• The skin of infants and children is much more sensitive than adult skin. Because essential oils are highly concentrated, essential oils should be used with caution in children, particularly those under the age 2, and only after consulting a pediatrician.

• Peppermint, eucalyptus, and some types of rosemary essential oils contain high amounts of menthol, which can cause slowed respiration in some children. Because of this, it is recommended that peppermint not be used on children under 6 years old; eucalyptus and rosemary should not be used on children under 10 years old.

• The American Academy of Pediatrics advises not to feed honey to children under the age of 1 year because of the risk of botulism.

HOMEMADE DOUBLE BOILER

No special gadgets or tools are needed to create the remedies and recipes in this book; you should be able to get by just fine with equipment you already own. One tool that you'll need for several recipes is a double boiler, which uses steam to gently melt delicate ingredients that could burn over direct heat. To make a double boiler, all you need is a saucepan and either a heatproof glass measuring cup (such as Pyrex) or a pint-size glass jar. The measuring cup or glass jar substitute for the top pan in store-bought double boilers. A measuring cup is a little easier to use because it has a handle, but a glass jar works fine, too. Because melted waxes and butters can make a mess that's hard to clean, I recommend designating a measuring cup or jar for all of your wax projects.

MATERIALS

Small saucepan

Canning jar ring

Heatproof glass measuring cup or pint-size glass jar

DIRECTIONS

Fill a small saucepan with 2 inches of water and bring to a low simmer. Place the canning jar ring in the center of the saucepan and set the measuring cup or jar on top of it. Place the ingredients you want to melt inside the glass container. The steam created from the simmering water, along with the layer of water between the saucepan and the cup, will gently heat your ingredients. Stir the ingredients occasionally with a wooden popsicle stick. Once your ingredients are melted, turn off the heat and carefully remove your glass container with the help of a pot holder or thick towel.

TIP To clean wax from glass cookware, preheat the oven to 200°F, then place the glass container on a rimmed baking sheet in the oven for 10 to 15 minutes, until the solid wax melts back to its liquid state. Once the wax has melted, carefully remove the container from the oven and wipe it clean with toilet paper. Since the wax and toilet paper are both biodegradable, you can prevent waste by composting the waxy toilet paper. Alternatively, once the jar has cooled, you can stick it in the freezer. The beeswax will harden and can then be easily removed and reused.

HOMEMADE BEESWAX MINIS

Several of the recipes in this book call for beeswax, which among its many uses works as a solidifying medium for salves, an emulsifier for cosmetics, and a hardener for balms. Because it's solid at room temperature and has a relatively high melting point, beeswax helps thicken and emulsify skin care products. It's also rich in vitamin A, promotes cell regeneration, is valued as an antiseptic and an antibiotic, and improves hydration while attracting moisture to the skin.

Beeswax can be purchased as a bar or as pastilles (or, sometimes, pellets). I like to buy a bar from a local beekeeper, not only because I love to support regional farmers and sustainable practices, but also because I can buy it in bulk without disposable packaging. The only disadvantage to buying bars over pastilles is they're a little harder to work with when it comes time to make a recipe. If, for example, you run out of lip balm and want to quickly whip up a tube, you'll have the extra step of having to grate the beeswax first. One way to get around this extra step—and save yourself some time—is to melt the bar of beeswax and pour it into small (teaspoon- or tablespoon-size) silicone molds. (A candy silicone mold is usually the right size.) Once the beeswax hardens, you can pop out the "minis" and store them in a glass jar. Although they're not as tiny as pastilles, they're small and easy to work with.

BEESWAX ALTERNATIVE

If you have an allergy to beeswax or would prefer a vegan alternative, candelilla wax makes an excellent substitute. Candelilla wax is derived from the leaves of a plant native to Mexico and the southwestern United States. Odorless and pale yellow in color, it's commonly used as a stabilizer and emulsifier in balms, creams, lotions, and salves. Candelilla has many of the same lubricating properties as beeswax but is much harder and less pliable. As a result, you will need to adjust recipes so you use half as much candelilla as you would beeswax.

FIERY CIDER

Fiery cider—vinegar infused with a bevy of immune-boosting herbs, fruits, and vegetables—is a beloved folk remedy and a must for the natural wellness cabinet. Often referred to as a "crossover" remedy, it reflects the ways our ancestors used food from their gardens to make medicine in their kitchens. Fiery cider serves as a cold-weather preparation to boost the immune system, stimulate digestion, and warm the body. Since it takes a few weeks to infuse, I suggest preparing your cider a month before you think you'll need it. I like to start a batch or two a month before the fall equinox so that it's ready in time for cold and flu season.

Traditional recipes for fiery cider vary widely according to the ingredients available per region and season. If you can't scare up all the ingredients for this particular recipe, fear not—you can use whatever you do have and still make a potent remedy. Since you're using this as medicine, whenever possible try to use organic ingredients that have not been treated with herbicides and pesticides.

If planning to serve this to children, I recommend omitting the serrano peppers.

INGREDIENTS

½ cup chopped fresh ginger

½ cup chopped fresh horseradish

½ cup chopped fresh turmeric

½ small onion, chopped

1 head garlic, chopped

2 serrano peppers, cut in half lengthwise

1 lemon, peeled, cut into 1-inch pieces

1 orange, peeled, cut into 1-inch pieces

2 or 3 fresh parsley sprigs

2 or 3 fresh thyme sprigs

2 or 3 fresh rosemary sprigs

1 tablespoon black peppercorns

1 tablespoon cayenne pepper

2 cinnamon sticks

2 cups apple cider vinegar, store-bought or homemade (page 34)

¼ cup raw honey, or to taste

DIRECTIONS

Combine all the ingredients except the honey in a clean quart-size glass jar. Make sure everything is fully submerged in the vinegar. Cover the jar with a lid. If using a metal lid, you can prevent corrosion by placing a piece of compostable parchment paper between the jar and the lid. Store the jar in a cool, dark place for 1 month and shake it a little each day. When ready, strain the vinegar and compost the scraps. Add the honey and whisk until it's well incorporated. Transfer the finished cider to a clean glass jar with an airtight lid and store in the refrigerator for up to a month.

TO USE If you feel a cold or flu coming on, take 1 to 2 tablespoons every 3 to 4 hours until you feel better. As a preventative, take 1 tablespoon a day. It can be taken straight or diluted in water or soup.

SHIITAKE HEALING SOUP

When my children were little, our pediatrician used to prescribe this soup at the onset of cold and flu symptoms. In addition to keeping us warm, it nourished us with vitally nutritious vegetables, herbs, and spices. Best of all, it contains shiitake mushrooms, which are packed with B vitamins, a host of minerals and enzymes, and a fleet of antibacterial, antiviral, and antifungal properties. Although it's been a decade since she first wrote the ingredients on a page of her prescription pad, I still turn to it when someone in our family starts to feel under the weather.

INGREDIENTS

4 carrots, chopped

3 celery ribs, chopped

1 bunch scallions, chopped

1 cup shiitake mushrooms, chopped

2 tomatoes, chopped

1 head garlic, chopped

1-inch piece fresh ginger, chopped

1-inch piece fresh turmeric, chopped

1 bunch fresh flat-leaf parsley, chopped

8 cups water or vegetable stock, store-bought or homemade (page 32)

Juice of 1 lemon, or to taste

1 teaspoon crushed red pepper (optional)

Salt and ground black pepper, to taste

DIRECTIONS

Combine the carrots, celery, scallions, mushrooms, tomatoes, garlic, ginger, turmeric, and parsley in a pot, add the water, and bring to a gentle boil over medium heat. Turn the heat to low and allow the soup to simmer for about an hour. Strain the soup (compost the solids), add the lemon juice and crushed red pepper (if using), and season with salt and black pepper to taste.

TO USE Sip throughout the day, or until you feel better.

IMMUNE-BOOSTING LEMON-GINGER TONIC

Whenever I feel a little "puny," as my grandmother would say, I pull out my juicer and treat myself to this invigorating tonic. The ginger is warming, stimulating, and decongesting; the lemon is astringent and high in vitamin C and bioflavonoids; and the turmeric helps the body deal with inflammation. To sweeten the tonic without adding a lot of sugar, I like to use Granny Smith apples. If I have cilantro, I include that as well, as it helps clean and extract toxins from the body. When it's all said and done, I "close the loop" and use the apple cores to make apple cider vinegar (page 34) and the lemon peels to make citrus all-purpose cleaner (page 74). **Makes about 2 cups**

INGREDIENTS

2 Granny Smith apples, unpeeled, chopped

2 lemons, peeled and chopped

2-inch piece fresh ginger, peeled

1-inch piece fresh turmeric, peeled

5 or 6 fresh cilantro sprigs (optional)

DIRECTIONS

Feed all the ingredients through the feed chute of a juicer. For maximum benefits and to prevent oxidation, drink within 24 hours.

TO USE I like to take 2-ounce shots throughout the day, although I've also been known to chug an entire bottle in one sitting. What can I say? I love this stuff.

ELDERBERRY SYRUP

Elder is esteemed as the queen of herbs or "the people's medicine chest." It's no wonder—as a powerful medicinal, it's played an important role in health and wellness for more than a thousand years. Elder is still highly revered in Europe, where it's used to make the continent's most popular herbal cold remedy. Medicinally, elder is used as an antioxidant and to support the heart, reduce inflammation, and improve vision. It's best known for its ability to boost and balance the immune system and quell coughs, colds, and flus. These days, it's often sold as syrups, jams, and medicinal wines. While you can certainly buy these products from natural food stores and local markets, you can just as easily prepare them yourself. My favorite way to prepare elderberry is in syrup form, also a favorite among the children in our home. It's made from dried elderberries, which you can buy at some natural grocery stores or online.

INGREDIENTS

2 cups water

½ cup dried elderberries

1 tablespoon minced fresh ginger

1 teaspoon ground cinnamon

½ teaspoon ground cloves (optional)

½ cup raw honey

DIRECTIONS

Pour the water into a medium pan. Add the elderberries, ginger, cinnamon, and cloves (if using). Bring the water to a boil over medium heat, then reduce the heat to low and let simmer for 45 minutes. Remove the pan from the heat and use the back of a spoon to press the berries to extract their juices. Strain the liquid through a fine-mesh strainer and compost the berries and pulp. Once the juice has cooled to room temperature, add the honey and whisk until it's well incorporated. Pour the syrup into a glass bottle or jar, seal with an airtight lid, and label and date the jar. Store in the refrigerator for up to 1 month. If you don't think you'll use it all, you can freeze some for later, either as syrup or as ice pops (see next recipe).

TO USE When unwell, take 1 to 2 tablespoons every 3 to 4 hours until you feel better. As a preventative, take 1 to 2 tablespoons a day.

ELDERBERRY ICE POPS AND GUMMIES

Though elderberry syrup tastes wonderful on its own, ice pops and gummies are two fun and easy ways to get this deeply nourishing medicine into children—and grown-ups, too! Elderberry ice pops are my favorite because they serve the dual function of boosting the immune system while soothing a sore throat.

ELDERBERRY ICE POPS

INGREDIENTS

Elderberry syrup (page 135)   *Fresh orange or apple juice, or tart black cherry juice*

DIRECTIONS

Put 1 tablespoon elderberry syrup in each ice pop mold and top it off with juice. The juice from one medium orange or one large apple is usually just the right amount per pop. Give it a swirl, freeze until firm, and enjoy!

TO USE One or 2 pops is the equivalent of one dose of elderberry syrup, so you can enjoy 1 pop every 3 to 4 hours when unwell, or 1 a day preventatively.

ELDERBERRY GUMMIES

INGREDIENTS

1¼ cups tart black cherry juice   *¼ cup elderberry syrup (page 135)*
¼ cup unflavored, grass-fed gelatin   *2 tablespoons raw honey*

DIRECTIONS

Pour the juice into a small saucepan and warm over medium heat. Add the gelatin and whisk briskly and constantly until the gelatin is completely dissolved. Remove the pan from the heat and add the elderberry syrup and honey. Whisk and mix well. Place silicone molds on a sturdy baking sheet, then spoon the mixture into the molds. Place the baking sheet with the molds in the refrigerator until firm, 30 to 60 minutes. Pop the gummies out of the molds and store for up to 2 weeks in an airtight container in the refrigerator.

TO USE Assuming the cavities of the mold hold about 1 tablespoon each, you can take 6 to 12 gummies every 3 to 4 hours when unwell, until you feel better.

ECHINACEA TINCTURE

Echinacea is one of the oldest and most commonly used herbs in the world. Its popularity comes as no surprise considering its effectiveness in boosting the immune system. According to research conducted in Germany, echinacea enhances the body's natural resistance to infection by increasing macrophage and T-cell activity, the body's first lines of defense against infection. It's also potent without having many, if any, side effects, which makes it safe for children and the elderly. It's commonly prepared as a tincture that can be taken to boost the immune system or ward off respiratory infections or sore throats. Echinacea is most effective when taken at the onset of symptoms.

INGREDIENTS

½ cup dried echinacea root   *1½ cups 80-proof vodka or brandy*

½ cup dried echinacea flowers

DIRECTIONS

Put the echinacea roots and flowers in a pint-size glass jar. Add the vodka; it should cover the herbs by a couple of inches. Cover the jar with a tight-fitting lid, shake well, and leave to steep in a cool, dark place, shaking daily, for 4 to 6 weeks—the longer you leave it, the more potent it will be. Strain the herbs from the liquid, compost the herbs, and pour the liquid into a clean glass dropper bottle. Store in a cool, dark place for up to 5 years.

TO USE If you feel a cold or flu coming on, take ½ teaspoon up to once every hour. Reduce the dosage as symptoms subside. The tincture can be taken straight or added to tea or water.

SAFETY TIPS Echinacea should be avoided if you are taking prescription drugs for heart disease or otherwise advised by your doctor.

Children under age 2 do not have fully developed livers and have a hard time breaking down alcohol. Before giving an alcohol-based tincture to a young child or someone who should avoid alcohol, add a drop of the tincture to a cup of boiling water. The alcohol will evaporate by the time the water is cool enough to drink.

LEMON-GINGER TEA

Ginger has a long history of use in traditional and alternative medicine. Often used to improve digestion and relieve nausea, it's also known to reduce inflammation, relieve a sore throat, clear congestion, ease aches and pains, treat migraines, and warm you from the inside out—a welcome quality when you've got the chills from being sick. I tend to use it most often during cold and flu season, particularly when I have congestion and a sore throat. I find the lemon and ginger stimulating and helpful at clearing sinuses, while the honey helps soothe a scratchy, raw throat. If I have homemade sage honey (page 146) in the cupboard, I use that to help with congestion.

INGREDIENTS

2-inch piece fresh ginger, peeled and grated

2 tablespoons fresh lemon juice, or more to taste

2 cups boiling water

Raw honey

DIRECTIONS

Put the ginger and lemon juice in a Thermos, then pour in the boiling water. Cap the Thermos, shake vigorously, and allow to steep for 15 to 30 minutes.

TO USE Strain 1 cup at a time into a mug, add honey to taste, and drink warm.

Top left: Lemon-Ginger Tea (above); top right: Sage Honey (page 146); bottom left: Marshmallow-Peppermint Digestive Tea (page 147); bottom right: Sweet Dreams Tea Blend (page 151)

LICORICE-THYME COUGH SYRUP

This syrup is a delicious way to ease a cough by ingesting concentrated doses of licorice, thyme, and ginger. The licorice and honey help reduce inflammation and soothe a sore throat; the thyme calms coughing spasms, clears chest congestion, and soothes a sore throat; and the ginger helps relieve congested coughs and stuffy sinuses.

INGREDIENTS

¼ cup dried licorice root

¼ cup dried thyme

2 tablespoons minced fresh ginger

4 cups filtered water

1 to 2 cups raw honey

DIRECTIONS

Combine the licorice, thyme, and ginger in a saucepan and add the filtered water. Over low heat, simmer the tea until the liquid has been reduced by half. Strain the tea, compost the solids, and pour the tea back into the pot. Add the raw honey and warm the mixture over low heat. Stir constantly until the temperature reaches 105°F on a candy thermometer (not higher, to avoid killing the enzymes in the honey). Turn off the heat and transfer the syrup to a clean bottle or jar. Label the jar with the name and date and refrigerate for up to 6 months.

TO USE For adults, take 1 tablespoon 3 or 4 times per day until symptoms subside. For children under age 12, take 1 teaspoon 2 or 3 times per day.

SAFETY TIPS Licorice should be avoided if you take prescription drugs for heart disease or are otherwise advised by your doctor.

According to the American Academy of Pediatrics, honey should not be given to children under age 1 because of the risk of botulism.

Consult a pediatrician before administering this syrup to children.

NATURAL VAPOR RUB

There's nothing worse than not being able to sleep because you can't breathe. Since commercial vapor rubs are often formulated with petroleum and parabens, I like to make a salve with essential oils that relieve coughing and congestion. Eucalyptus is antibacterial, anti-inflammatory, and an expectorant, which makes it ideal for breaking up congestion; peppermint is antibacterial, anti-inflammatory, and soothing; lavender is calming and can help promote sleep; tea tree is antimicrobial and effective at fighting pathogens; and lemon is antiviral and great for soothing colds, coughs, and other respiratory problems. Because eucalyptus and peppermint should not be taken by children, I created a separate formula for little ones using cedarwood and frankincense.

INGREDIENTS FOR ADULTS

¼ cup coconut oil

¼ cup shea butter

*2 tablespoons beeswax
or 1 tablespoon candelilla wax*

20 drops eucalyptus essential oil

20 drops peppermint essential oil

10 drops lavender essential oil

5 drops tea tree essential oil

5 drops lemon essential oil

INGREDIENTS FOR CHILDREN (UNDER 10 YEARS OLD)

¼ cup coconut oil

¼ cup shea butter

*2 tablespoons beeswax
or 1 tablespoon candelilla wax*

8 drops cedarwood essential oil

8 drops tea tree essential oil

4 drops lavender essential oil

4 drops frankincense essential oil

DIRECTIONS

Pour 2 inches of water into the bottom of a double boiler (see page 127 for how to make your own double boiler) and bring to a simmer over medium heat. Combine the coconut oil and shea butter in the top of the double boiler and heat until they melt. Remove the top pan from the heat and allow to cool for 5 minutes. Add the essential oils, mix thoroughly, then pour the mixture into a glass or tin container. Allow to cool for about an hour, then cover and store in a cool, dry place.

TO USE Apply and massage onto the chest to relieve coughing and congestion.

SAFETY TIP Eucalyptus essential oil should not be used by children under age 10. Peppermint essential oil should not be used by children under age 6.

SAGE HONEY

An herbalist could exhaust herself listing the medicinal uses of sage. Although it's usually considered a culinary herb, it works just as well in the medicine cabinet. Because of sage's ability to tighten and tone swollen tissues, one of my favorite ways to use it is for cough relief. Infused in honey, it's easy to make and even easier to administer, and it makes a wonderful alternative to over-the-counter cough syrups. In one randomized, double-blind trial, researchers compared the effects of a sage and echinacea extract on sore throats to a spray made up of chlorhexidine and lidocaine and found that the herbal extract was slighly more effective at reducing symptoms. When needed, I give it to my children by the spoonful, drink it myself in warm water with lemon, or add it to tea.

INGREDIENTS

½ cup dried sage   *1½ cups raw honey*

DIRECTIONS

Place the dried sage in a clean pint-size glass jar and pour in the honey. Cover and seal the jar and allow the honey to infuse in a dark place for 2 to 4 weeks—the longer it infuses the stronger it will be. When ready, strain the honey through a sieve into a clean jar and seal with an airtight lid. Label the jar with the name and date and store in a cool, dark place until ready to use. It will last indefinitely.

TO USE For a sore throat, spoon 1 teaspoon sage honey into a mug. Bring 1 cup water to a near boil, pour over the honey, and add the juice of half a lemon. Sip and enjoy!

SAFETY TIPS According to the American Academy of Pediatrics, honey should not be given to children under the age of 1 year because of the risk of botulism. Because of its drying effects, sage should not be used during pregnancy or while breastfeeding.

MARSHMALLOW-PEPPERMINT DIGESTIVE TEA

Marshmallow has been used for thousands of years by cultures around the world from the Romans and Arabs to the Chinese, Egyptians, and Syrians. As food, it was eaten and revered as a root vegetable. As medicine, it was boiled with honey to make a rich confection used to treat sore throats and stomach aches. Marshmallow contains a substance called mucilage, which works to soothe inflamed tissues in the respiratory, digestive, and urinary tracts. This recipe contains peppermint as well, not just because it adds a refreshing and delicious flavor, but also because therapeutically, it's said to reduce inflammation and calm digestive upsets. Notably, this tea works just as well for sore throats as it does for tummy aches and indigestion. For sore throats, I love to combine it with the sage honey from page 146.

INGREDIENTS

2 tablespoons dried marshmallow root   *2 cups room-temperature water*

2 teaspoons dried peppermint leaf

DIRECTIONS

Combine the marshmallow and peppermint in a quart-size glass jar. Pour the water over the herbs. Seal the jar tightly and allow the mixture to steep for 2 to 3 hours. Strain the liquid and compost the herbs.

TO USE Drink ½ cup 2 or 3 times a day to relieve an upset stomach or sore throat.

SAFETY TIP Consult a pediatrician before giving this tea to children.

DIGESTIVE BITTERS

Sweet, sour, salty, umami, and bitter: These are the five flavors that our taste buds are primed to identify. Today, with the preference for sweet, salty processed foods, bitter flavors have all but disappeared from our plates and palates. Some herbalists attribute current-day digestive problems to what they call a "bitter deficiency" in our culture's diet. It makes sense, considering the benefits of bitter foods. When consumed, they engage and excite the digestive system by stimulating the production of saliva, gastric juices, and bile to balance the appetite and prime digestion. Taking bitters regularly is said to soothe heartburn and indigestion, calm upset stomachs, relieve nausea, stimulate detoxification, and support healthy skin. Although the traditional way to incorporate bitters into one's diet is through real food—namely nutrient-dense greens like arugula, chicory, dandelion, and endive—you can also add liquid bitters to your meals. A liquid bitter is prepared just like a tincture, but with bitter herbs as the plant material. It can be sipped straight, mixed with a beverage, or incorporated in a fancy cocktail. Below is one simple recipe.

INGREDIENT

1 tablespoon chopped dandelion root

1 tablespoon chopped burdock root

1 tablespoon chopped fresh orange, peel removed

2 teaspoons grated fresh ginger

½ cinnamon stick, crushed

1 cup 80-proof vodka

DIRECTIONS

Combine the dandelion, burdock, orange peel, ginger, and cinnamon in a pint-size glass jar. Pour in the vodka and make sure that all of the ingredients are completely submerged. Stir well and seal with an airtight lid. Label the jar with the name, plants used, and date. Store the jar at room temperature in a cool, dark place to infuse for 4 to 6 weeks—the longer you leave it, the more potent it will be. Strain the liquid and transfer it to an amber dropper bottle.

TO USE Add 1 teaspoon bitters to water, sparkling water, juice, or a cocktail and take 15 to 30 minutes before meals.

STRESS RELIEF TEA BLEND

A delicious blend with soothing nervines (herbs that support the nervous system), this tea will help you relax at the end of a stressful day. One ingredient is lemon balm, an herb the Renaissance physician and alchemist Paracelsus called the "elixir of life"—perhaps because of its effectiveness in relaxing the nervous system, promoting sleep, and calming the digestive system. Another ingredient is skullcap, which acts as a sedative and nerve tonic to relieve anxiety, stress, and tension. For convenience, I like to make enough of the dried blend for 8 cups of tea. You can certainly double or triple it if you think you'll use it often.

INGREDIENTS

2 tablespoons dried lemon balm

2 tablespoons dried chamomile

2 tablespoons dried skullcap

1 tablespoon dried lavender buds

1 tablespoon dried passionflower

DIRECTIONS

Combine the herbs in a 4-ounce glass jar and mix well. Seal the jar, label and date it, and store in a cool, dark place for up to 6 months.

TO USE Make an infusion by adding 1 tablespoon herb blend to 1 cup boiling water. Allow the tea to steep for 15 to 30 minutes—the longer it steeps, the stronger it will be. After infusing the tea, strain and sip.

SAFETY TIP Consult a pediatrician before giving this tea to children.

SWEET DREAMS TEA BLEND

If you have trouble sleeping, you'll love this tea blend combining herbs that soothe the nervous system and support sleep. Because herbs work best when used repeatedly, I suggest mixing a whole jar of it so that you can easily make a cup of tea every night before bed. One batch of this will make 8 cups of tea. You can double or triple it if you think you'll use it often.

INGREDIENTS

3 tablespoons dried chamomile

2 tablespoons dried lemon balm

1 tablespoon dried catnip

1 tablespoon dried oatstraw

1½ teaspoons dried passionflower

¾ teaspoon dried hop flowers

¾ teaspoon dried valerian

DIRECTIONS

Combine the herbs in a 4-ounce glass jar and mix well. Seal the jar, label and date it, and store in a cool, dark place for up to 6 months.

TO USE Make an infusion by adding 1 tablespoon herb blend to 1 cup boiling water. Allow the tea to steep for 10 to 15 minutes—the longer it steeps, the stronger it will be. After infusing the tea, strain and sip about an hour before bedtime.

SAFETY TIP Consult a pediatrician before giving this tea to children. I like to give my own children plain chamomile tea to help them relax before bedtime.

SWEET DREAMS HONEY

On its own, honey is potent medicine. When you infuse it with herbs, it becomes a super medicine with the potential to deliver healing properties without the bitter taste of tinctures and teas. Inside my wellness cabinet, I keep a medley of herbal honeys, including sage honey (page 146) for sore throats, turmeric honey for inflammation, and garlic honey for immune support. But my favorite is sleepy time honey. Infused with herbs that settle the nervous system and promote sleep, it makes a perfect addition to sweet dreams tea (for adults; see page 151) or plain chamomile tea (for children).

INGREDIENTS

1 tablespoon dried chamomile flowers   *1 tablespoon dried lemon balm*

1 tablespoon dried lavender flowers   *2 cups raw honey*

DIRECTIONS

Put the herbs in a clean quart-size glass jar. Pour in the honey, making sure the herbs are fully submerged. Screw on a tight-fitting lid and place in a cool, dark place for 2 to 4 weeks—the longer you leave it, the more potent it will be. Check on the honey daily. If the herbs float to the top, turn the jar upside down to resubmerge them. After 2 to 4 weeks, pour 1 inch of water into a small saucepan. Remove the lid from the jar of honey and stand the jar in the water. Turn the heat to medium and warm the honey until melted. Take care not to let the water boil—otherwise, the high temperature will destroy the honey's enzymes. Once melted, strain the honey, transfer to a clean glass jar, seal with an airtight lid, and store in a cool, dark place indefinitely.

TO USE Add ½ to 1 tablespoon honey to 1 cup warm Sweet Dreams Tea (page 151) or plain chamomile tea.

SAFETY TIP According to the American Academy of Pediatrics, honey should not be given to children under age 1 because of the risk of botulism.

BOO-BOO OIL AND BALM

One of my favorite ways to use herbs is to turn them into infused oils and balms. The process isn't hard, but it can take time if you make them the slow way by cold infusion. I like to begin infusing oils at the end of August when the growing season has ended and my kitchen is overflowing with fresh herbs and flowers. By fall equinox, I usually have a well-stocked medicine cabinet for the colder months. This particular recipe is for a balm and oil I use in lieu of Neosporin for dry skin and all manner of scrapes, cuts, bites, and sores. Its therapeutic properties come in large part from calendula, a flower with anti-septic and anti-inflammatory properties that promotes cell repair and growth. When I turn the oil into a balm, I also add essential oils that aid in cleaning, soothing, and healing wounds, such as chamomile, frankincense, lavender, or tea tree.

INGREDIENTS

¾ cup dried calendula flowers

1 cup cold-pressed olive oil

3 tablespoons beeswax or
1½ tablespoons candelilla wax

10 to 15 drops essential oil (optional)

DIRECTIONS

1. Put the calendula flowers in a clean pint-size glass jar. Pour in the olive oil, submerging the calendula by at least 1 inch. Stir well, cover with a tight-fitting lid, and place in a cool, dark place to infuse for 4 to 6 weeks—the longer you leave it, the more potent it will be. Once the oil is infused, strain it through a fine-mesh sieve or cheesecloth, compost the herbs, and transfer the oil to a clean glass jar. You can use the oil as is or make a balm.

2. To make a balm, pour 2 inches of water into the bottom of a double boiler (see page 127 for how to make your own) and bring to a simmer over medium heat. Combine the infused oil and wax in the top of the double boiler and heat until the wax melts completely. Remove the top pan from the heat, stir in the essential oil, and carefully pour into containers. Allow to cool and set for an hour, then cover and store in a cool place for up to a year.

NOTE You can adjust the consistency of your balm by re-melting it in the double boiler and adding more olive oil if you want a softer balm or more wax if you want a firmer one.

PEPPERMINT LIP BALM

Lip balm is one of the easiest and most useful products to make at home. I like to infuse mine with peppermint essential oil, but you could certainly use other ones. Just be careful to avoid phytotoxic oils, which can become toxic when exposed to sunlight; common phytotoxic essential oils include bergamot, lemon, lime, mandarin, and orange.

This recipe makes about 3 ounces of balm, which can be poured into metal tins, glass jars, or cardboard lip balm tubes (I purchase mine from Etsy). One batch fills six ½-ounce tins or nine ⅓-ounce tubes. That's a lot of lip balm, so I usually keep a few tubes in my wellness cabinet to use throughout the year and gift the others for holidays and birthdays. You can adjust the recipe to make fewer tins or tubes if you wish.

INGREDIENTS

2 tablespoons organic coconut oil

2 tablespoons shea butter

2 tablespoons grated beeswax or 1 tablespoon grated candelilla wax

10 drops essential oil

DIRECTIONS

Pour 2 inches of water into the bottom of a double boiler (see page 127 for how to make your own) and bring to a simmer over medium heat. Combine the coconut oil, shea butter, and beeswax in the top of the double boiler and heat until they melt. Remove the top pan from the heat and add the essential oil. Mix thoroughly and transfer to clean containers. If you have an eyedropper or a pipette, it makes transferring the mixture to containers much easier. Allow the balm to set for 30 to 60 minutes, then store in a cool, dry place for up to a year.

NOTES You can adjust the consistency of your lip balm by re-melting it in the double boiler and adding more coconut oil for a softer balm or more wax for a firmer one.

To make a tinted lip balm, add 2 tablespoons beetroot powder or hibiscus powder along with the essential oils.

SAFETY TIP Peppermint essential oil should not be used in children under age 6. Safer alternatives for young children include chamomile, lavender, tea tree, vetiver, and ylang-ylang.

HEADACHE RELIEF BALM

When my husband gets tension headaches, I love helping him find alternatives to over-the-counter medications. What has worked best to help relieve symptoms is to dilute specific essential oils and apply them to his temples, forehead, and wrists. Because he travels a lot and isn't likely to bring essential oils and carrier oils with him, I add them to a salve that he can easily carry with him in a lip balm tube or metal tin. This recipe makes three 1-ounce containers of headache balm. You can adjust it according to how many tins or tubes you wish to make.

INGREDIENTS

2 tablespoons coconut oil

2 tablespoons shea butter

2 tablespoons grated beeswax
or 1 tablespoon candelilla wax

20 drops peppermint essential oil

10 drops lavender essential oil

10 drops frankincense essential oil

5 drops rosemary essential oil

DIRECTIONS

Pour 2 inches of water into the bottom of a double boiler (see page 127 for how to make your own double boiler) and bring to a simmer over medium heat. Combine the coconut oil, shea butter, and wax in the top of the double boiler and heat until they melt. Remove the top pan from the heat and add the essential oils. Mix thoroughly and transfer to clean containers. If you have an eyedropper or a pipette, it makes transferring the mixture to containers much easier. Otherwise, pouring with a steady, slow hand works just fine. Allow the balm to set for 30 to 60 minutes, then store in a cool, dark place.

TO USE Apply a small amount of the balm to temples, back of head, shoulders, and behind ears. Gently massage into skin and breathe its aroma.

NOTE You can easily adjust the consistency of your balm by re-melting it in the double boiler and adding more coconut oil if you want a softer balm or more wax if you want a firmer one.

SAFETY TIP Peppermint essential oil should not be used in children under age 6 and rosemary essential oil should not be used in children under age 10.

OATMEAL-CALENDULA ITCH RELIEF BATH

Adding oatmeal, calendula flowers, and baking soda to a warm bath can soothe dry, itchy, or inflamed skin with conditions like eczema, chicken pox, poison ivy, or mosquito bites. The oatmeal and calendula are anti-inflammatory, while the baking soda raises the pH of the skin and helps reduce itchiness.

INGREDIENTS

½ cup oatmeal   *¼ cup baking soda*

¼ cup dried calendula flowers   *5 drops lavender essential oil*

DIRECTIONS

Grind the oatmeal into a fine powder in a food processor or blender. Combine all the ingredients in a medium bowl and mix well. Transfer the mixture to a nylon stocking or thin cotton dress sock and secure it with a knot.

TO USE Add the sock to a warm bath and soak for 30 minutes. Squeeze the sock periodically to release as much of the oatmeal starch as possible. Compost the ingredients, rinse the stocking well, and line-dry for reuse.

NATURAL BUG SPRAY

Summer is a joyous time of year. My childhood memories of summer are peppered with images of hiking, biking, camping, swimming—and, unfortunately, spraying bug spray all over my body! Now, years later, I'm the mother of a very sweet child—so sweet the mosquitos love her almost as much as I do. Fortunately, one of my favorite DIYs is this simple and effective bug spray that works on mosquitos, gnats, flies, and other warm-weather bugs. If you have concerns about putting essential oils directly on your children's skin, you can spray their clothes, hats, socks, and shoes instead; see the safety tip as well.

This recipe is extremely versatile. If you don't have all of the essential oils listed, simply use some variation of the ones you have or substitute them for other insect-repelling essential oils, such as lemongrass, vetiver, and patchouli. All in all, you'll want to use a little less than 100 drops of essential oils per 8-ounce bottle.

INGREDIENTS

½ cup witch hazel extract

20 drops citronella essential oil

20 drops lemon eucalyptus essential oil

20 drops geranium essential oil

10 drops lavender essential oil

10 drops rosemary essential oil

10 drops cedarwood essential oil

5 drops tea tree essential oil

½ cup water or apple cider vinegar, store-bought or homemade (page 34)

½ teaspoon vegetable glycerin

DIRECTIONS

Pour the witch hazel extract into a spray bottle. Add the essential oils, apple cider vinegar, and vegetable glycerin.

TO USE Shake well before using and apply as often as needed. Keep out of eyes, nose, and mouth.

SAFETY TIP Eucalyptus and rosemary should not be used in children under age 10. If making this for young children, you can omit those essential oils and instead double up on the citronella and cedarwood.

SIMPLE ITCH AND STING RELIEF REMEDIES

Some of the best home remedies for relieving itchy, inflamed bug bites are incredibly simple and can be made from ingredients found in your backyard or kitchen cupboard.

ALOE VERA GEL. Soothes and relieves itchy, inflamed skin. To use, just dab a bit of gel on the wound. You can buy gel from the store or remove it from the leaf of a houseplant.

APPLE CIDER VINEGAR OR LEMON JUICE. Acid helps neutralize the alkaline venom of insects like yellow jackets, hornets, and wasps. To use, dip a clean cloth in apple cider vinegar or lemon juice and apply to the wound.

BAKING SODA. As a base, helps neutralize the acidic venom of ants and bees and other biting, stinging insects (other than yellow jackets, hornets, and wasps). To use, make a paste of baking soda and water and apply it to the wound for 30 to 60 minutes.

BENTONITE CLAY. Raises the temperature of the skin, increases circulation, and draws out toxins. To use, make a paste of clay, aloe, and water and apply to itchy, inflamed areas for 30 minutes.

FRESH PLANTAIN. Draws out toxins and functions as a natural painkiller, anti-inflammatory, and antiseptic. To use, find a leaf from an area away from roads, railroad tracks, or areas treated with pesticides, chew it for 30 seconds, then apply it like a poultice to the wound.

LAVENDER OR TEA TREE ESSENTIAL OIL. Can be applied to the skin to reduce inflammation and prevent infection. To use, mix 1 to 3 drops essential oil with 1 teaspoon sweet almond oil and apply to the affected area.

PEPPERMINT-LAVENDER SUNBURN RELIEF OIL

This peppermint-lavender essential oil blend is a simple remedy for mild sunburns. The lavender is analgesic and works to numb the pain, nurture the skin, and help regenerate new skin cells; the peppermint is cooling, anti-inflammatory, and analgesic. For convenience, I like to keep the oil in a glass roll-on bottle that I can carry with me in my purse or backpack.

INGREDIENTS

2 tablespoons jojoba or sweet almond oil

3 drops (for ages 15 and under) or 7 drops (for ages 15 and over) lavender essential oil

3 drops (for ages 6 to 15) or 7 drops (for ages 15 and over) peppermint essential oil

DIRECTIONS

Blend the oils together and transfer to a glass roll-on bottle.

TO USE Gently apply to all areas that have been burned or exposed to too much sun. Apply as needed for 2 to 3 days.

SAFETY TIP Peppermint essential oils should not be used on children under age 6. Instead, combine 2 tablespoons of jojoba or sweet almond oil and 6 drops of lavender essential oil.

ALOE VERA GEL FOR WOUND AND BURN RELIEF

Aloe vera was the first plant I saw my grandfather use medicinally. If my grandmother burned her finger on a hot pan or my brother came home with a minor sunburn, my grandfather would tear a leaf off an aloe plant and apply its fresh gel to their wounds. Not only is aloe gel soothing and pain relieving, but it also contains a high concentration of anthraquinones, which are known to promote rapid healing and tissue repair. Among its many healing properties, it can reverse blisters and prevent scarring and tissue damage. It's useful for wounds and burns, as well as insect bites, stings, rashes, poison ivy, and poison oak. (For a severe burn, however, see a doctor.)

INGREDIENTS

Aloe vera plant

DIRECTIONS

Depending on the size of the burn or wound, cut a small or large succulent leaf from an aloe vera plant. Be sure to leave some of the leaf intact so that it can continue to grow from the base of the mother plant. Using a sharp knife, slice open the leaf horizontally to expose the gel. Scoop out the inner gel with a spoon and apply it directly to the burn, wound, or rash. Repeat several times a day until the burn or wound heals. If you cover the area with a bandage, be sure to use one that will allow the skin to breathe.

TIP If you have removed a large leaf, you can puree the gel in a blender and store it in a glass jar in the refrigerator for several weeks.

ARNICA SALVE FOR BRUISES AND SPRAINS

Arnica oil is a must for the home apothecary. It's the herb to turn to immediately after an injury to reduce shock and speed healing. An alpine flower native to Europe, Central Asia, and Siberia, arnica eases the pain and inflammation of sore muscles, sprains, strains, and bruises and is commonly used by athletes to soothe the aches of sports injuries and speed recovery after training. It's restricted to topical application, as it can cause serious side effects when taken internally. I like to prepare it as a salve that can be applied easily and quickly in the event of injury.

INGREDIENTS

¾ cup dried arnica flowers

1 cup cold-pressed organic olive oil

2 tablespoons beeswax or
1 tablespoon candelilla wax

DIRECTIONS

1. Put the dried flowers in a clean pint-size glass jar. Add the olive oil, making sure the flowers are submerged by at least an inch. Stir to combine, cover with a tight-fitting lid, and place in a cool, dark place for 4 to 6 weeks—the longer you leave it, the more potent it will be. Strain the oil through a fine-mesh strainer or cheesecloth. Compost the herbs.

2. To make the salve, pour 2 inches of water into the bottom of a double boiler (see page 127 for how to make your own double boiler) and bring to a simmer over medium heat. Combine the infused oil and beeswax in the top of the double boiler and heat until the wax melts. Remove the top pan from the heat and carefully pour the mixture into containers. Allow to cool and set for an hour, then cover and store in a cool, dark place for up to a year.

TO USE Apply and gently massage over bruises, sprains, or strains. Use as needed for up to a few days, until pain subsides.

NOTE You can adjust the consistency of your salve by re-melting it in the double boiler and adding more oil if you want a softer salve or more beeswax if you want a firmer one.

SAFETY TIPS Arnica should never to be taken internally and should not be used on broken skin, where it can cause irritations and rashes. It is also not recommended for pregnant or breastfeeding women.

Do not use on children under 8. Instead, use the boo-boo balm (page 154).

NATURAL BATH
AND BODY

If you're shopping with canvas bags, composting food waste, using homemade cleaning supplies, and making your own cough syrup, you're more than ready for a natural bath and body routine. In some cases, this may consist of buying products made with natural, nontoxic ingredients. In other cases, you may find yourself making your own using simple ingredients from your kitchen cabinets. Either way, it can have a huge effect when it comes to your health. According to the Environmental Working Group, on average, most Americans use nine personal care products a day, exposing themselves to a total of 126 chemical ingredients. Unfortunately, in the United States, these products are underregulated, as the Food and Drug Administration has no authority to require health studies and testing before cosmetics are sold. Perhaps more disturbing is the fact that many of the ingredients used in cosmetics sold in the United States have been banned in other countries and have been linked by scientists to serious health problems.

Aside from eliminating potentially hazardous chemicals, a natural bath and body routine is a great way to reduce waste—just think of all the plastic containers currently residing in your bathroom. In my experience, eliminating toxic toiletries also led to minimizing waste. Not only did I swap excessively packaged products for simple, homemade recipes, but I also substituted disposable products with reusable ones. Plastic toothbrushes were replaced by bamboo ones; bottled shampoos and conditioners were swapped with unpackaged bars and vinegar rinses. Not surprisingly, the same products that are good for you are also good for the planet.

As I made changes to my bath and body routine, I also changed how I perceived natural beauty. Although I'd never been one to purchase a lot of products or wear much makeup, I did buy lotions and creams to prevent aging. I didn't like to admit it, but as I grew older I grew more determined to avoid the wrinkles, lines, spots, and blemishes that can come with age. That changed when a health issue forced me to make significant changes to my lifestyle. As I started taking better care of myself—consuming clean foods, eating mostly fruits and vegetables, eliminating sugar and caffeine—my skin improved dramatically. The dark circles that had been under my eyes since childhood disappeared. My complexion became rosy and bright. For the first time in ages, I felt like I looked a little radiant and, as it turned out, I didn't need specially formulated products. What I needed—what I'd been missing—was wellness.

Now I approach my bath and body routine holistically. A lot of it happens in the kitchen or in the garden, and definitely in the way I eat, drink, and sleep. The rest happens in the bathroom, where I've mostly ditched commercial products for homemade ones. When making my own products, my goal is always to keep things simple, nontoxic, nourishing, and low-waste. In this section, I share some of my favorite bath and body recipes for everything from basic toiletries to nourishing face washes and indulgent herbal bath teas. Depending on your access to bulk items, you may have to buy a few staple ingredients in plastic packaging, but remember that a little bit goes a long way and will last a long time. Most of the recipes in this section can be prepared using ingredients from your backyard, garden, or wellness cabinet—which is to say, they are healthy, healing, and nourishing, for both you and the planet.

ZERO-WASTE BATHROOM SWAPS

After the kitchen, the bathroom is the second most wasteful part of most homes. As such, it's a great place to eliminate unnecessary packaging by replacing disposable items with reusable ones and shopping for products that are sustainably packaged or, better yet, package-free. Look at it as an opportunity to simplify your beauty routine, avoid harmful or toxic chemicals, and take control of the products you put in and on your body, as well as the ones that inevitably slip back into the environment. Remember that making a swap doesn't mean throwing away what you currently own but rather using it until it has served its purpose and *then* replacing it with a healthier, more sustainable product and routine.

DISPOSABLE AND/OR TOXIC	REUSABLE AND/OR NONTOXIC
Plastic toothbrush	Bamboo toothbrush
Lip balm	Homemade lip balm, stored in a tin or cardboard tube
Plastic-packaged lotion	Homemade lotion, body butter, or lotion bars
Plastic-bottled shampoo	Shampoo bar, refillable bottles, or the no-poo method
Plastic-bottled conditioner	Conditioner bar, refillable bottles, or apple cider vinegar
Plastic-packaged dry shampoo	Homemade dry shampoo
Plastic dental floss	Water pick or silk floss in glass jar
Cotton swabs with plastic applicator	Cotton swabs with wooden applicator
Paper tissues	Cloth handkerchiefs
Plastic-tubed toothpaste	Homemade toothpaste or commercial in a glass jar or recyclable metal tube
Commercial mouthwash	Homemade mouthwash
Plastic razor	Stainless steel safety razor
Plastic comb and hair brush	Wooden comb and hairbrush
Plastic nail brush	Wooden nail brush
Plastic exfoliator brush	Loofah sponge
Plastic hair ties and pins	Biodegradable hair ties and wooden hair pins
Tampons	Silicone menstrual cups
Disposable menstrual pads	Reusable cloth menstrual pads, period panties
Disposable makeup remover pads	Reusable makeup remover pads
Traditional makeup remover	Coconut oil or olive oil
Commercial facial toner	Apple cider vinegar or homemade toner
Commercial perfume	Aromatherapy essential oil blends
Liquid body soap	Unpackaged bar soap
Antibacterial soap	Bar soap, homemade hand sanitizer
Plastic-wrapped toilet paper	Paper-wrapped, recycled/bamboo toilet paper or a bidet
Conventional deodorant	Homemade or commercial, zero-waste deodorant
Individually packaged bath bombs	Homemade bath bombs
Commercial blushers and bronzers	Homemade, plant-based blushers and bronzers
Plastic shower curtain	Natural fiber shower curtain
Plastic travel bottles	Silicone travel bottles
Plastic travel soap box	Tin soap box (or a repurposed metal Altoids container)
Plastic trash can	Natural fiber trash can or metal compost bucket with lid

TOOTHPASTE TWO WAYS

The first DIY toiletry product I ever experimented with was toothpaste. After trying a variety of homemade recipes, I eventually settled on these two, which left my mouth feeling fresh and clean and passed muster with my dentist. The difference between the two formulations is that one includes baking soda, which helps neutralize the pH of the mouth while gently removing plaque, and one excludes it since baking soda can be an irritant to some people.

Both recipes contain bentonite clay, coconut oil, and xylitol. The bentonite clay promotes tooth remineralization and reduces the pH in the mouth. It also binds to toxins and draws them out of the body. The coconut oil is antimicrobial and prevents candida, which contributes to tooth decay. The xylitol, a natural sweetener that can be purchased online and in most natural grocery stores, helps maintain a neutral pH in the mouth and blocks cavity-causing bacteria from attaching to teeth. I recommend trying both recipes to see which one works best for you.

VERSION 1 INGREDIENTS

5 tablespoons powdered bentonite clay, or more as needed

⅓ cup filtered water, or more as needed

2 tablespoons organic, unrefined coconut oil, melted

1 tablespoon xylitol

6 drops peppermint essential oil or, for children under age 6, peppermint extract

VERSION 2 INGREDIENTS

3 tablespoons powdered bentonite clay, or more as needed

¼ cup filtered water, or more as needed

2 tablespoons baking soda

2 tablespoons organic, unrefined coconut oil, melted

1 tablespoon xylitol

6 drops peppermint essential oil or, for children under age 6, peppermint extract

DIRECTIONS

Combine all the ingredients in a bowl and use a wooden spoon to mix thoroughly into a smooth paste (avoid metal utensils, as they will deactivate the electrical charge of the clay). Add more clay or water, as needed, to achieve the right consistency, which should be like a thick paste for the first recipe and a whipped paste for the second one. When well mixed, transfer the paste to a container (I like a glass jar for the first one and a silicone tube for the second one) and store at room temperature. If storing in glass jars, I recommend making one for each family member to prevent cross-contamination of germs.

SAFETY TIP Peppermint essential oils should not be used in children under age 6.

PEPPERMINT MOUTHWASH

I've seen and tried some lovely homemade herbal mouthwash recipes, but they can be a bit costly and time-intensive, involving multiple tinctures that can take up to 4 weeks to make. When it comes to some DIY staples, I just want simple and easy, and this mouthwash fits the bill. The aloe vera helps soothe inflammation, bleeding gums, and gingivitis; the baking soda alkalizes the mouth and makes it less hospitable to bacteria; and the xylitol adds sweetness and helps prevent cavities. I don't add essential oils for young children, since they might swallow them, but for adults, I like to add a few drops of tea tree, peppermint, and clove essential oils. Tea tree and peppermint are believed to combat bacteria and inflammation; clove is anti-inflammatory, analgesic, and helpful for soothing pain, including toothaches and sore throats.

INGREDIENTS

¼ cup aloe vera juice or the gel of 3 leaves from a medium-size plant

1 cup distilled water

2 teaspoons baking soda

2 teaspoons xylitol

4 drops peppermint essential oil or, for children under age 6, peppermint extract (optional)

2 drops tea tree essential oil (optional)

2 drops clove essential oil (optional)

DIRECTIONS

Mix all the ingredients in a glass bottle and seal with an airtight lid.

TO USE Shake well before each use. Swish with 3 tablespoons of mouthwash for 1 to 2 minutes. Do not swallow.

SAFETY TIP Peppermint essential oils should not be used for children under age 6.

DEODORANT TWO WAYS

If you're looking to reduce single-use packaging and/or avoid putting questionable ingredients on your body, homemade deodorant might be your entrée into the world of bath and body DIYs. To save you a weekend's worth of thumbing through natural wellness books, magazines, and blogs, I'm sharing two of my favorite natural deodorants here. One is a liquid roll-on that uses witch hazel extract as its base; the other is a solid, oil-based recipe that looks and feels like a traditional stick of deodorant.

Aside from these two deodorants, there's also the option of neutralizing body odor by cleaning your underarms with apple cider vinegar or witch hazel extract. Apple cider vinegar is naturally acidic, with antimicrobial properties, while witch hazel extract is an astringent that excels at removing excess oil. I like to keep a little basket with a bottle of one or the other along with a stack of reusable face pads. When I step out of the shower or if I feel like I need a little freshening up, I douse a pad in apple cider vinegar or witch hazel extract and wipe my underarms clean. Some people like to do this in addition to using the natural deodorants, since it neutralizes the pH of the underarm area and inhibits bacterial growth.

WITCH HAZEL EXTRACT ROLL-ON DEODORANT

INGREDIENTS

½ teaspoon baking soda or sea salt

1½ tablespoons alcohol-free witch hazel extract

1½ teaspoons organic vegetable glycerin or aloe vera gel

12 drops lavender or tea tree essential oil

DIRECTIONS

Using a small funnel, pour the baking soda, witch hazel extract, glycerin, and essential oil into a glass roll-on bottle. Attach the cap, shake well, and use as needed.

TIP If you're sensitive to baking soda, use sea salt instead.

HOMEMADE DEODORANT STICK

INGREDIENTS

2 tablespoons shea butter

2 tablespoons cocoa butter

1 tablespoon beeswax

1 tablespoon sweet almond oil

1 teaspoon vitamin E oil

2¹/₂ tablespoons arrowroot powder

2 tablespoons kaolin or bentonite clay

15 drops essential oil (tea tree, peppermint, or lavender)

DIRECTIONS

Pour 2 inches of water into the bottom of a double boiler (see page 127 for how to make your own double boiler) and bring to a simmer over medium heat. Combine the shea butter and cocoa butter in the top of the double boiler and heat until they melt. Add the beeswax and stir with a wooden popsicle stick until it melts. Add the almond oil and mix well. Remove the top pan from the heat and quickly add the vitamin E oil, arrowroot powder, and clay. Stir until the dry ingredients are completely dissolved. Add the essential oil, then carefully pour into a cardboard deodorant tube (available on Etsy), a tin container, or a glass jar. Allow to set, put on the lid, and store at room temperature. When ready to use, simply rub under your arms or apply with your hands.

HAND SANITIZER

Studies show that antibacterial soap provides no extra germ-fighting benefits and, even worse, exposes you and your family to potentially harmful substances. Other studies show that children exposed to dirt have healthier, more robust immune systems than their squeaky-clean peers. In our house, we abide by the belief that the best way to stay healthy is to play in the dirt and wash up with nothing more than a little soap and water. But when soap and water aren't available—say, because we're at the park or hiking—I use this gentle aloe vera–based hand sanitizer. Unlike commercial hand sanitizers, this one uses only nurturing plants and essential oils to kill bacteria. It also smells better than the stuff they sell at the supermarket!

INGREDIENTS

⅓ cup pure aloe vera gel

1 tablespoon witch hazel extract

¼ teaspoon vitamin E oil

10 drops tea tree essential oil

5 drops lavender essential oil

DIRECTIONS

Combine all the ingredients in a small bowl. Mix together with a fork and then transfer the mixture to a travel-size silicone squeeze tube.

ESSENTIAL OILS THAT NOURISH THE SKIN

CARROT SEED Antioxidant; renews skin quickly.

CHAMOMILE Treats eczema, acne, rosea, and inflammation.

CLARY SAGE Fights signs of aging and reduces puffiness.

CYPRESS Acts as an stringent; heals pimples and skin eruptions.

FRANKINCENSE Restores damaged skin; tones and tightens.

GERANIUM Conditions and balances oil production; minimizes appearance of wrinkles.

LAVENDER Increases circulation and soothes skin irritations.

PEPPERMINT Softens, tones, and calms skin; remedies dermatitis, inflammation, and oily skin.

ROSEMARY Antiseptic; helps with dermatitis, oily skin, and acne; promotes toned skin.

TEA TREE Antifungal and antibacterial; treats cuts and scrapes, as well as acne and pimples.

YLANG YLANG Treats oily, acne-prone skin; stimulates cell growth.

HERBAL FACE WASH

A natural skin care routine begins with a good facial cleanser. This wash combines herb-infused water, castile soap, and a moisturizing oil to help remove impurities, makeup, and excess sebum while soothing skin irritations and reducing fine lines and wrinkles. You can personalize it by adding essential oils that accommodate your particular skin type and needs. As a cleanser, it works best as the first step in your skin care routine, followed by any other treatments you might use, such as a scrub or mask, toner, serum, and moisturizer.

INGREDIENTS

1 tablespoon dried calendula

1 tablespoon dried chamomile

1 tablespoon dried lavender

1 cup boiling water

1 cup liquid castile soap

1 tablespoon jojoba or sweet almond oil

5 drops essential oil (see opposite)

DIRECTIONS

Prepare the herb-infused water by combining the herbs in a pint-size glass jar. Pour the boiling water over the herbs and steep for 30 to 45 minutes. Strain out the herbs (and compost them), then combine the herb-infused water, castile soap, moisturizing oil, and essential oil. Transfer the mixture to a 16-ounce glass bottle, seal tightly, and mix well.

TO USE Apply a small amount of cleanser to your wet face and massage into the skin using circular motions, avoiding your eyes. Rinse well with warm water.

TIP To prevent contamination, infuse the herbs in distilled water and/or store the final face wash in the refrigerator.

OATMEAL FACE SCRUB

Homemade facial scrubs are a great place to start if you're new to DIY skin care. Not only are they easy to make using familiar, inexpensive ingredients, they're also an important step in a healthy skin care routine. Facial scrubs can slough off dead skin cells, soften skin, and reduce the appearance of pores, fine lines, and wrinkles. Ideally, they should be used 1 to 3 times a week, after cleaning the face and before applying a toner or moisturizer. Although scrubs can be made with a variety of exfoliants such as sugar, salt, and baking soda, I like to use a base of oatmeal, which has been used for thousands of years to gently cleanse, exfoliate, heal, and moisturize the skin. It's safe for all skin types and is excellent at soothing sensitive skin. **Makes ½ cup powder for the scrub**

INGREDIENTS

¼ cup old-fashioned rolled oats

¼ cup raw almonds

2 tablespoons dried chamomile or lavender buds (optional)

Jojoba or sweet almond oil

Lavender essential oil

DIRECTIONS

Grind the oats, almonds, and herbs in a food processor until finely ground. Sift through a mesh screen to remove large pieces, and store the powder in a sealed glass jar until ready to use.

TO USE Combine 1 tablespoon of jojoba and 1 drop of lavender essential oil in a small bowl and mix well. Add 2 tablespoons of the powder to the bowl and mix well to create a thick, spreadable paste. Massage the paste into the face using gentle, circular motions, then rinse with lukewarm water.

Top left: Oatmeal Face Scrub (above); top right: Rose-Lavender Facial Toner (page 188); bottom left: Queen of Hungary's Water (page 189); bottom right: Rejuvenating Facial Serum (page 190)

CLAY FACE MASK

Not only do clay face masks help exfoliate the skin, but they also unclog pores, extract excess oil, and rebuild damaged skin tissue. This recipe calls for bentonite clay, which, when activated with a liquid, acts like a magnet that binds to positively charged heavy metals, bacteria, and other impurities. It also mineralizes the skin by infusing it with calcium, magnesium, potassium, and selenium. This mask works best when applied once or twice a week, after a facial cleanser or scrub and before a toner.

INGREDIENTS

1 tablespoon powdered bentonite clay

1 tablespoon raw honey

1 tablespoon apple cider vinegar, store-bought or homemade (page 34), or rose water, store-bought or homemade (page 185)

2 drops frankincense, lavender, or tea tree essential oil (optional)

DIRECTIONS

Combine all the ingredients in a small bowl and mix well to form a paste.

TO USE Apply the paste evenly to the face using gentle, circular motions, let it sit for 10 to 15 minutes, then rinse with lukewarm water.

HOMEMADE ROSE WATER

Pure rose water is distilled from rose petals and has been used for thousands of years, both for its lovely scent and for medicinal and culinary purposes. As an herb, rose is cooling, soothing, anti-inflammatory, and astringent. As a skin tonic, it tightens pores, smooths fine lines, balances the skin's pH, and slows the aging process. Like other floral waters, rose water is used in a variety of bath and beauty products, including as a facial toner, to soothe tired or puffy eyes, to help remove makeup, and as an ingredient in lotions, creams, face masks, hair rinses, shampoos, sprays, and perfumes. While you can certainly purchase rose water, you can also make it yourself if you have access to fresh, organic roses. The best way to harvest them is to snip the flower heads of newly opened blooms early in the morning, before the sun has baked away their oils. If you choose to buy rose petals instead, look for organic ones to ensure your final product is pesticide-free.

INGREDIENTS AND MATERIALS

Large canning jar ring

Small heat-safe bowl (stainless steel or glass)

6 to 8 cups fresh, organic roses

Distilled water

2 to 3 trays full of ice cubes

Turkey baster or large serving spoon

DIRECTIONS

1. Position the canning jar ring in the center of a stockpot. Place the heat-safe bowl on top of the ring.

2. Put the roses in the stockpot, scattering them around the jar ring and bowl. Continue to layer the roses until they're at about the height of the bottom of the bowl. Pour the distilled water into the stockpot around the sides of the bowl, submerging the rose petals. The water level should be at least a couple of inches below the rim of the bowl. Place the lid on the pot upside down, so that the handle in the center is pointing toward the bowl.

continued

3. Turn the heat to medium-high and bring the water to a boil. Once the water is boiling, reduce the heat to a low simmer and fill the inverted pot lid with several handfuls of ice. You've now created a home still: As the water boils, steam will rise, hit the top of the pot lid, condense because of the cold temperature of the ice, flow to the center of the lid, and drop into the bowl. As the ice melts, use a turkey baster or large serving spoon to remove the cold water. Continue removing water and adding ice for 20 minutes or so, or until most of the water around the base of the bowl is gone. Remove the pot from the heat and allow it to cool to room temperature. Carefully remove the lid and transfer the rose water from the bowl to a clean glass jar. Seal with an airtight lid and store in a cool, dark place for up to a year.

NOTE You can use this process to make any type of floral water, including chamomile, geranium, lavender, lemon balm, lemon verbena, rosemary, thyme, and peppermint.

ROSE-LAVENDER FACIAL TONER

Applied after cleansing and exfoliating, facial toners remove excess oils, hydrate the skin, and tighten and tone pores. They can be made from floral waters, herbal infusions, apple cider vinegar, witch hazel extract, or even vodka. The following simple recipe is very gentle and can be reworked in countless, creative ways by substituting different floral waters or essential oils according to your skin type, needs, and preferences. It can be applied before your serum and moisturizer, but also throughout the day to hydrate the skin.

INGREDIENTS

¼ cup rose water, store-bought or homemade (page 185)

2 tablespoons witch hazel extract

1 tablespoon aloe vera gel

10 drops lavender essential oil

DIRECTIONS

Combine all the ingredients in a bowl and mix well. Using a funnel, transfer the toner to a 4-ounce glass bottle.

TO USE Shake well. Apply the toner to a clean reusable cloth pad. Massage it into the skin in gentle circular motions, being sure to avoid the eyes. Allow to air-dry, or pat dry.

QUEEN OF HUNGARY'S WATER

This recipe is slightly more involved than the facial toner on page 188, but it is certainly worth the extra effort. An ancient folk remedy, it's said to have been created by an alchemist in the 1300s to restore the youthful appearance of the aging Queen Elisabeth of Hungary. Legend has it the 25-year-old Duke of Lithuania was so smitten with the queen's appearance, he proposed marriage even though she was 70 years old! In other folklore, it's considered a special formula created by the Romani as an antidote for a wide range of cosmetic and medicinal issues. Regardless of its true origin, there's no doubt that Queen of Hungary's water is a lovely astringent for all skin types. Not only does it tone and tighten pores, but it normalizes the skin's pH and soothes skin irritations. **Makes about 4 cups**

INGREDIENTS

6 tablespoons dried lemon balm

4 tablespoons dried lavender flowers

4 tablespoons dried chamomile flowers

4 tablespoons dried rose petals

3 tablespoons dried calendula flowers

1 tablespoons dried rosemary leaf

1 tablespoons dried peppermint leaf

1 tablespoons dried sage leaf

2½ cups apple cider vinegar, store-bought or homemade (page 34)

2 cups rose water, store-bought or homemade (page 185), or witch hazel extract

5 drops lavender essential oil

DIRECTIONS

Combine the herbs in a clean quart-size glass jar. Pour in the apple cider vinegar and make sure the herbs are submerged. Seal the jar and allow the mixture to infuse for 4 to 6 weeks—the longer you leave it, the more potent it will be. Strain out the herbs and transfer the liquid to another clean, quart-size glass jar. To make the toner, mix 2 cups herb-infused vinegar with 2 cups rose water or witch hazel extract and add the essential oil. Store in a cool, dark place indefinitely.

TO USE Shake well, and apply the toner to a clean reusable cloth pad. Massage it into the skin in gentle circular motions, being sure to avoid the eyes. Allow to air-dry, or pat dry.

REJUVENATING FACIAL SERUM

Facial serums are lightweight moisturizers that contain a high concentration of nourishing ingredients. As part of a natural skin care routine, they're best applied after cleansing and toning and before moisturizing the skin. For a carrier oil, this recipe uses rose hip seed oil, which penetrates the skin quickly, hydrates and plumps the skin, promotes collagen production, and reduces the appearance of fine lines and wrinkles. It also includes a combination of essential oils known for their ability to repair and renew the skin: Myrrh fights free radicals and reduces cellular inflammation; helichrysum reduces scars, acne marks, and spots; frankincense promotes the growth of new skin cells and reduces the appearance of fine lines and wrinkles; and geranium contains antioxidants and helps treat eczema, dermatitis, and psoriasis.

INGREDIENTS

2 tablespoons rose hip seed oil

3 drops myrrh essential oil

3 drops helichrysum essential oil

3 drops frankincense essential oil

3 drops geranium essential oil

DIRECTIONS

Pour the rose hip seed oil into a small glass bottle. Add the essential oils, put on the lid, and incorporate the ingredients by gently rolling the bottle between the palms of your hands.

TO USE Apply a coin-size drop to the face, then massage it into the skin using small, soft upward strokes.

CALENDULA BODY BUTTER

Come winter, when everything from my hands to my heels feels dry and chapped, I like to make this calendula-infused body butter. Unlike lotions and creams, which contain water, body butters nourish and protect the skin by sealing in moisture and creating a barrier between the skin and the elements. For this reason, body butters are best suited to super-dry skin that needs protection from cold air and low humidity.

INGREDIENTS

¼ cup dried calendula flowers

⅓ cup fractionated coconut oil, melted

⅓ cup grapeseed oil

½ cup cocoa butter

2 tablespoons shea butter

10 drops lavender essential oil

DIRECTIONS

1. Make an herbal infusion by putting the calendula flowers in a clean pint-size glass jar. Pour in the coconut and grapeseed oils, being sure to submerge the flowers by at least an inch. Stir well, cover with a tight-fitting lid, and place in a sunny spot to infuse for 4 to 6 weeks—the longer you leave it, the more potent it will be. Strain the herbs, compost the scraps, and transfer the calendula oil to a clean glass jar. You should have about ½ cup.

2. Pour 2 inches of water into the bottom of a double boiler (see page 127 for how to make your own double boiler) and bring to a simmer over medium heat. Combine the infused calendula oil (if you have less than ½ cup, top it off with more grapeseed oil), cocoa butter, and shea butter in the top of the double boiler and heat until the butters melt. Pour the mixture into a small bowl. Add the essential oil, mix well, and set the bowl in the refrigerator for a few hours to solidify.

3. Transfer the solid mixture to the bowl of a stand mixer and beat on high speed until it has the consistency of a creamy, fluffy butter. Refrigerate the body butter for 10 to 15 minutes, then spoon it into glass jars with airtight lids. Store in a cool, dark place for up to a year.

LEMON-ROSEMARY LOTION BARS

Lotion bars are a fun DIY that look a bit like a bar of soap but otherwise work just like a moisturizer. Although solid at room temperature, they melt just a little when you rub them against your warm skin. Unlike their liquid counterparts, lotion bars are incredibly convenient. When it comes to making them, you get to skip the difficult step of emulsifying oils and water, and when it comes time to use them, they're clean, compact, and portable. I like to pop a bar in a tin container and take it with me wherever I go—including through airport security, where I've been asked to surrender liquid lotion more times than my well-prepared husband wants you to know. They also make unique gifts for friends, neighbors, family, and teachers, wrapped up in fabric scraps tied with twine.

INGREDIENTS

5 tablespoons grated beeswax or 3 tablespoons grated candelilla wax

3 tablespoons cocoa butter

3 tablespoons shea or mango butter

5 tablespoons sweet almond oil

10 drops lemon essential oil

5 drops rosemary essential oil

DIRECTIONS

Pour 2 inches of water into the bottom of a double boiler (see page 127 for how to make your own double boiler) and bring to a simmer over medium heat. Combine the wax and cocoa butter in the top of the double boiler and heat until they melt. Add the shea butter and almond oil and mix with a wooden popsicle stick. Remove the top pan from the heat and stir in the essential oils. Carefully pour the mixture into silicone soap molds and allow to harden at room temperature. Once set, pop the lotion bars out of the molds and store in tin containers or glass jars at room temperature.

TO USE Rub the lotion bar on dry areas, such elbows, hands, feet, heels, or knees, and massage into skin until absorbed.

SAFETY TIP Rosemary essential oil should not be used on children under 10 years old. If you plan to use these bars on children, omit that ingredient and just use lemon essential oil.

ROSE BODY CREAM

If body butters and lotion bars are too thick or greasy for your liking, or if you are not looking to treat or heal extremely dry skin, you might prefer making and using a cream. Like lotions, creams tend to be lighter, less greasy, and more easily absorbed than body butters. The difference between butters and creams is that butters are a mixture of natural butters and carrier oils, whereas creams (and lotions) involve emulsifying water and oil. Because of their water content, creams tend to rehydrate the skin quickly but also have a higher risk of growing mold. To prevent that, I suggest using distilled rather than tap water and making small batches you'll use quickly. You can also store your cream in the refrigerator for extra protection. Here is a simple starter recipe inspired by herbalist Rosemary Gladstar's technique for making the perfect cream.

INGREDIENTS

⅔ cup rose water, store-bought or homemade (page 185), or distilled water

⅓ cup aloe vera gel

2 to 10 drops essential oil (lavender, rose, Roman chamomile, and sandalwood are all good choices)

1 teaspoon vitamin E oil

¼ cup grapeseed oil

½ cup sweet almond oil

⅓ cup shea butter

1 tablespoon grated beeswax

DIRECTIONS

1. Combine the rose water, aloe vera gel, essential oil, and vitamin E oil in a small bowl and whisk together. These are your water-based ingredients.

2. Pour 2 inches of water into the bottom of a double boiler (see page 127 for how to make your own double boiler) and bring to a simmer over medium heat. In the top of the double boiler, combine the grapeseed oil, sweet almond oil, shea butter, and beeswax (your oil-based ingredients) and heat until melted. Mix well and remove the top pan from the heat. Transfer the mixture to a large bowl and stir frequently until it cools to room temperature. It should become thick, creamy, and semi-solid.

3. Transfer the oil mixture to a blender and blend on the highest setting. Slowly and steadily begin to add the water-based ingredients through the hole in the blender lid, allowing the water molecules to emulsify with the oils. The lotion will slowly begin to thicken. When the blender begins to cough and choke, and the cream looks like buttercream frosting, turn off the blender. You can slowly add more water (although you may not need it all), beating it in by hand with a spoon, but be careful not to over-beat it—the cream will thicken as it cools. Once cooled, spoon the cream into glass jars and store in a cool area or the refrigerator for up to 3 months.

HERBAL HAIR RINSE

If you're not familiar with the benefits of apple cider vinegar as a hair rinse, you're in for a real treat. In addition to removing buildup of hair products, it helps balance the hair's pH, clean the scalp, boost scalp circulation, condition hair, treat hair loss, and soothe dry, itchy scalp and dandruff. Infusing the vinegar with herbs adds a host of other benefits, from strengthening hair to promoting growth and reducing dandruff. Fresh herbs are best, but dried will work, too. If you find the smell of apple cider vinegar overpowering, you can add your favorite essential oil to mask the strong odor.

INGREDIENTS

2 or 3 small handfuls fresh or dried herbs (see opposite)

2 cups apple cider vinegar, store-bought or homemade (page 34)

5 to 10 drops essential oil (optional)

DIRECTIONS

Put the herbs in a quart-size glass jar. Pour in the apple cider vinegar and make sure the herbs are submerged. Place the lid on the jar, with a piece of compostable parchment paper between the jar and lid to prevent corrosion. Set the jar in a warm spot and leave to infuse for 4 to 6 weeks—the longer you leave it, the more potent it will be. When ready, strain and compost the herbs, add the essential oil (if using), and transfer the vinegar to a clean glass jar. The concentrated vinegar will store indefinitely, but you'll need to prepare the rinse before each wash.

TO USE Prepare the hair rinse by diluting the vinegar with water: Start with a base of somewhere between ½ cup and 1½ cups concentrated vinegar, depending on your hair length. Then for oily hair, dilute 1 part vinegar with 4 parts water; for normal hair, dilute 1 part vinegar with 5 parts water; for dry hair, dilute 1 part vinegar with 6 parts water (you may need to experiment with these ratios to find the best dilution for your hair type). Transfer the diluted rinse to a jar or spray bottle. Wash your hair as usual, then tilt your head back and spray or douse your hair with the rinse. Take care to avoid the eyes. Massage the rinse into your scalp and hair, leave it in for a few minutes, then rinse with water.

HERBS FOR HERB-INFUSED HAIR RINSE

BASIL Helps the body eliminate toxins and heavy metals; promotes hair growth.

CALENDULA FLOWERS Helps soothe scalp issues; enhances blond hair.

CHAMOMILE Soothes the scalp; enhances blond hair.

COMFREY Moisturizes dry scalp and hair.

HORSETAIL Rich in silica; strengthens hair; promotes hair growth.

LAVENDER Increases circulation; promotes hair growth; calms inflammation; soothes scalp irritations.

NETTLES Rich in vitamins and minerals; nourishes the scalp; stimulates hair growth.

OATSTRAW Rich in silica and vitamins A, C, and E.

PARSLEY High in iron and vitamin C; strengthens hair.

PEPPERMINT Antibacterial; antifungal; stimulates hair growth; soothes scalp issues.

ROSEMARY Increases scalp circulation; promotes hair growth; strengthens hair; fights dandruff.

HERBAL BATH TEA COMBOS

CALENDULA AND CHAMOMILE Reduces stress and softens and soothes the skin.

CHAMOMILE, LEMON BALM, AND HOPS Relieves stress and induces restful sleep.

CHAMOMILE, ROSEMARY, AND EUCALYPTUS Promotes relaxation and relieves symptoms of cold and flu.

EUCALYPTUS, PEPPERMINT, AND THYME Refreshes, revitalizes, and eases congestion and sore muscles.

HOPS AND HYSSOP Brings about restful sleep.

LAVENDER, CHAMOMILE, AND PEPPERMINT Soothes stress and rejuvenates the mind.

LAVENDER AND ROSE PETALS Promotes relaxation.

PEPPERMINT AND ROSEMARY Eases mind and body fatigue.

SAGE AND LEMON BALM Helps clear the head.

HERBAL BATH TEA

Herbal bathing provides an opportunity to relax and slow down while enjoying the medicinal properties of herbs. The earliest use of herbal baths dates to 1500 BCE in India, and it was also used for hygienic and medical purposes by the ancient Egyptians, Babylonians, Assyrians, and Hebrews. Hippocrates developed a method of treating disease through the use of water, which became common throughout Greece and, eventually, Rome, where people regularly convened in bath houses for water massage and aromatic therapies. Today, many doctors and other health practitioners tout herbal bathing for relieving tension, soothing sore muscles, and stimulating circulation, with a good soak conferring the benefits of warm water and the medicinal properties of herbs as they're slowly absorbed by your skin. You can customize an herbal bath according to your particular needs. Depending on which herbs you use, an herbal bath can be relaxing or stimulating.

INGREDIENTS

¼ cup dried herbs (see opposite)

DIRECTIONS

Fill a small muslin tea bag with dried herbs. (If you don't have a muslin tea bag, put the herbs on a piece of cheesecloth or cotton fabric and secure the corners of the fabric with a rubber band or piece of twine. A clean cotton sock works well as a bag, too.)

TO USE Hook or tie the sachet of herbs under the tub spout so that the water runs through the herbs as the bathtub fills. Once the bath is drawn, remove the pouch and let it float in the bathwater. Squeeze the bag occasionally to release the botanical essences. Soak in the bath for 15 to 20 minutes. At the end of bath, compost the herbs, rinse the bag, line-dry, and use again.

BATH BOMBS

There was a period in early motherhood when the only way I could lure my young children to the bath was by enticing them with a bath bomb. I'd essentially dangle one in front of them and walk slowly to the bathroom, leading them to a tub full of warm water. I'd drop the little ball into the tub and watch them leap after it as it fizzed and popped away in the water. As if that weren't enough, because they were made with Epsom salts and calming essential oils, those little bath bombs played a critical role in calming my children and readying them for bed. I must have purchased 20 commercial bath bombs before I finally tried making my own. They were a tough DIY project to get right—I ruined at least three batches and almost gave up—but eventually I discovered a recipe that works and am very happy to share it with you. You will need round metal bath bomb molds; depending on how many molds you have, you may need to mold the bath bombs in batches. These bath bombs are a staple at our house now and find their way into just about every gift basket I prepare for friends, family, neighbors, and teachers. If you choose to gift them, a lovely low-waste way to wrap them is in scrap fabric secured with yarn or twine. **Makes approximately 6 medium-size bath bombs**

INGREDIENTS

1 cup baking soda

1/2 cup cornstarch or arrowroot powder

1/2 cup food-grade citric acid

1/2 cup Epsom salts

1 1/4 teaspoons coconut oil, melted

1 to 1 1/2 teaspoons filtered water

12 to 15 drops lavender essential oil

continued

DIRECTIONS

1. Combine the baking soda, cornstarch, citric acid, and Epsom salts in a medium bowl. Whisk well to remove clumps. In a separate bowl, combine the coconut oil, filtered water, and essential oil. Slowly add the wet ingredients to the dry ingredients while stirring constantly. If the mixture starts to fizz, slow down a bit. To test whether the mixture is ready for the molds, squeeze a bit in the palm of your hand. If it sticks together, it's ready. If it's still dry and powdery, it needs more water. Add a drop or two at a time and continue to test.

2. Fill half of a bath bomb mold with the mixture. Pack it tightly until it's overflowing just a little. Fill the other half of the mold and press the two together. Gently remove one side of the mold by pulling it upward while lightly twisting it from side to side. Set the bath bomb down on a tray, mold-side down. Allow the bath bomb to dry for 1 to 2 hours.

3. Gently remove the bath bomb from the other half of the mold. The best way to remove it is to invert the bath bomb so that the mold is on top. If the bath bomb crumbles when you try to remove it, pack it back into the mold and give it more time to dry. If the whole thing crumbles apart, just start the process over. It can take a little practice to successfully remove the bath bomb from the mold. Once the bath bomb is removed from the mold, allow it to air-dry completely for 8 to 10 hours. Store bath bombs in a clean glass jar with an airtight lid.

RELAXING HERBAL BATH SALTS

Bath salts have been used for centuries to relax achy muscles, reduce inflammation, detoxify the body, calm the mind, and moisturize and soothe dry skin. If you're in the mood for a simple salt soak, a cup of Epsom salts and 5 to 10 drops of essential oils will do the trick. But if you're looking for a slightly more luxurious experience, or a lovely gift idea, this herbal bath salt recipe is second to none. I like adding dried flowers from my garden or wellness cabinet, both for their fragrance and aesthetics—my favorites being calendula, chamomile, lavender, and rose. If you wish to avoid having to clean up flower petals, either leave them out of the recipe completely or add them separately in a muslin bag so they can steep in the bathwater.

INGREDIENTS

2 tablespoons sweet almond or jojoba oil

5 drops lavender essential oil

5 drops cedarwood essential oil

2¹/₂ cups Epsom salts

1¹/₂ cups Himalayan pink salt

¹/₂ cup baking soda

¹/₂ cup dried flowers (optional)

DIRECTIONS

In a small bowl, combine the sweet almond oil and essential oils and mix thoroughly. Combine the salts, baking soda, and the dried flowers (if using) in a large bowl, add the oils, and mix again. Transfer the mixture to a large glass jar with a tight-fitting lid.

TO USE Add 1 to 1½ cups of bath salts to a warm bath. Swish the water with your hand until the salts are completely dissolved. Soak for 20 to 30 minutes.

CITRUS PEPPERMINT FOOT SOAK

A foot soak is one of my favorite ways to treat myself at the end of the day. Although there are lots of possibilities when it comes to choosing herbs and oils, my favorite recipe combines citrus fruits and peppermint essential oil. A refreshing and uplifting blend, it's also packed with aromatic oils and antimicrobial properties that help disinfect and deodorize the feet.

INGREDIENTS

2 tablespoons sweet almond oil

5 drops peppermint essential oil

5 drops tea tree essential oil

1 gallon warm ("bath temperature") water

¼ cup baking soda

2 or 3 citrus fruits (orange, lemon, and/or lime), sliced

DIRECTIONS

In a small bowl, combine the sweet almond oil and essential oils and mix thoroughly. Pour the warm water into a large basin. Add the baking soda to the basin of water and stir well to dissolve it. Add the oils and citrus fruits.

TO USE Take a seat, open a book, listen to relaxing music, and soak your feet for 10 to 15 minutes.

HERBAL MASSAGE OIL

Massage is one of the best ways to relax the mind, body, and spirit. When paired with soothing botanicals, the experience becomes all the more therapeutic. Although you can make massage oils quickly using essential oils, I prefer making them the slow, old-fashioned way with dried herbs. As always, if you don't have all of the herbs called for in this recipe, you can leave out the ones you don't have and double up on the others.

INGREDIENTS

2 tablespoons dried calendula

2 tablespoons dried chamomile

2 tablespoons dried lavender

2 tablespoons dried roses

¾ cup sweet almond oil

5 to 10 drops lavender essential oil

DIRECTIONS

Combine the herbs in a clean pint glass jar. Pour in the almond oil, making sure the herbs are submerged by at least an inch. Stir to combine and seal with an airtight lid. Place the jar in a cool, dark place to infuse for 4 to 6 weeks—the longer you leave it, the more potent it will be. Strain and compost the herbs, add the essential oil, and store in a clean glass jar with an airtight lid.

PLANT-BASED BLUSH

If you're interested in making plant-based makeup, blush is a fun and easy place to start. I recommend starting with ½ teaspoon arrowroot powder for the base and then adding ¼ teaspoon of each plant constituent at a time. The following recipe is my go-to formula, but you can experiment with different color combinations until you find one that suits your mood and skin tone. In terms of plants and colors, my favorites are alkanet root (for magenta), beetroot (for burgundy), cinnamon (for brown), cocoa powder (for brown), ginger (for yellow), hibiscus (for pink), madder root (for rusty red), rose petals (for red or pink), and turmeric (for deep orange). You can purchase most of these powders online or at a regular or natural grocery store, or you can try making them yourself. To do so, simply dehydrate the plant part you wish to use, then blend it in a high-speed blender until it's powdery. I've done this for a few plants and found the process fun, but I'm also glad I can buy them ready-made online!

INGREDIENTS

1 teaspoon arrowroot powder   *1 teaspoon hibiscus powder*

½ teaspoon unsweetened cocoa powder

DIRECTIONS

Combine the ingredients, mix well, and store in a small glass jar or metal tin for up to a year.

TO USE Apply with a blush brush.

EASY MAKEUP REMOVER

This two-ingredient makeup remover gets the job done gently and without synthetic chemicals, fragrances, or other harsh ingredients. Combine 2 tablespoons jojoba oil and 2 tablespoons witch hazel extract in a 2-ounce glass jar. Cap and shake well before each use. To use, place a few drops on your fingers or a reusable facial round and gently apply to skin to remove makeup.

KITCHEN
GARDEN

When I think of my grandparents, the first thing that comes to mind is the fresh fruits, vegetables, and herbs from their garden. In the summers, we would hardly be out of the car before my grandfather was asking if we'd like to harvest a watermelon. He took great pride in his heirloom tomatoes and was known for sharing them with his friends and neighbors. As if that weren't enough, every Sunday, my grandmother would make lunch for the whole family—aunts, uncles, cousins, and all—serving dishes made with ingredients from her garden.

It's no surprise that, as an adult, my happiest memories include the times I've worked in a garden. Even when I didn't have the space or time for a large kitchen garden, at the bare minimum I kept a few pots of herbs or raised beds, sometimes with nothing more than a handful of cherry tomato and basil plants. When I lived in Guinea for two years, I had my first large-scale garden. After the first year of subsisting off cassava, rice, and raw milk, I decided to build a 16-bed garden and grow foods that weren't available in my community. It was quite an endeavor, particularly because there was no running water and I had to pull every drop from a 25-foot-deep well. Luckily I had the time and motivation to do it. It helped that I was young and energetic, too! I grew carrots, peppers, onions, garlic, greens, corn, squashes, and root vegetables. I ate well that season and learned the joy of sharing food. Every time someone came to my garden, I made sure they left with the ingredients for a salad. It was joyful and gratifying, to say the least.

When my family settled into our forever home in the Chicago area a few years ago, I was finally able to start my dream garden. It's not as large as the one I had in Guinea, but it meets our needs. What makes it special is that we set it up less than ten paces from our back door. It's a true kitchen garden, one from which I gather veggies, herbs, and flowers as easily if they were in my refrigerator or kitchen cabinets.

It probably goes without saying that my kitchen garden has been the ultimate tool in creating a simple, natural, low-waste home. After all, what could be more natural, simple, and waste-free than eating from your own backyard? We are able to grow our produce without chemicals or pesticides and, of course, without packaging. And importantly, it brings the natural home full circle. Imagine how complete it feels to grow your own herbs and then use them to make your own food, medicine, and bath and body products. In this section, I share some of my favorite ways (so far—I'm always experimenting and learning!) to use vegetables and herbs from my garden, as well as a few tips to make it a hardy, strong, diverse, and joyful space. There's a little bit for everyone too—several of these activities and recipes are good fun to do and make with children. My daughter has all but taken ownership of the garden, including growing and harvesting vegetables, saving seeds, feeding birds, and planting perennials for beneficial bugs, birds, and butterflies.

NEWSPAPER SEEDLING POTS

Newspaper seedling pots are a welcome surprise for the low-waste gardener. They're easy and affordable to make using newspapers right out of the recycling bin and, unlike plastic seed trays and pots, they're completely biodegradable. **Makes 3 pots**

MATERIALS

1 sheet of newspaper   *Seeds of your choice*

6-ounce can or spice jar   *Waterproof tray*

Seed-starting soil

DIRECTIONS

1. Fold the newspaper in half crosswise so you have a two-sheet stack. Cut it into thirds lengthwise to create 3 strips, each having 2 layers.

2. Place the can on its side on the newspaper, leaving 1 to 2 inches of newspaper hanging past the bottom of the can.

3. Tightly roll the newspaper around the can until you reach the end of the newspaper.

4. While holding the end of the newspaper with one hand, use your other hand to fold the edge of the newspaper down over the can, working your way around it until all the edges are crimped down. Flip the can right side up and press the can against a table to tighten the folds on the bottom of the pot.

5. Slide the can out of the newspaper pot. Don't worry if the pot feels flimsy; it will become surprisingly sturdy once filled with soil and water. Repeat with the other two newspaper strips.

6. Fill your newspaper pots with soil, plant your seeds, and store in a waterproof tray until ready to transplant to the garden. Water seeds daily.

7. When your seedlings are ready to be transplanted, plant the entire seedling pot in the soil.

BACKYARD COMPOSTING BASICS

According to the US Environmental Protection Agency, 30 percent of what Americans throw away is made up of food and yard waste. Although some food waste is inevitable, it's not really waste if you follow nature's example and recycle it back to the earth. After all, in nature, nothing gets wasted. A leaf falls from a tree and immediately begins the process of decomposing until it turns into the soil that feeds the very tree from which it fell. We can emulate this natural cycle in our own lives by composting food scraps, biodegradable materials, and yard waste.

If you've set up a low-waste kitchen and are collecting food scraps, you might as well compost them to make some "black gold" for the garden. Here are eight steps for setting up a successful backyard composting system.

CHOOSE A COMPOST BIN OR CREATE A PILE. A compost bin or an open pile will work. Bins have the advantage of keeping things neat and contained, while keeping out rodents and other critters. You can buy a bin or make one yourself.

CHOOSE A LOCATION FOR YOUR COMPOST. The best locations are flat, well drained, and easily accessible. In cool climates, place compost in a sunny spot with shelter to protect it from freezing cold winds. In warm, dry climates, place the bin or pile in a shadier spot to keep it from drying out too much.

UNDERSTAND THE CONCEPT OF BROWNS AND GREENS. There are two main ingredients in any compost pile: carbon-rich ingredients and nitrogen-rich ingredients. The carbon group, or "browns," includes materials like leaves, hay, paper, cardboard, sawdust, nut shells, and wood chips. The nitrogen group, or "greens," includes fruit and vegetable scraps, fresh grass clippings, coffee grounds, fresh herbs, and eggshells. The art of composting rests on balancing these groups.

CREATE A SYSTEM FOR COLLECTING KITCHEN SCRAPS. Have a system for collecting kitchen scraps, whether it be a compost bucket, an old slow cooker with a lid, or a large bowl you keep in the freezer to keep foods from rotting and smelling in the house. See page 217 for a list of foods and materials that can and cannot be composted.

COLLECT AND STORE BROWN (CARBON-RICH) MATERIALS. Create a system for collecting and storing brown materials to keep them dry—for example, in a brown paper yard waste bag in a shed or garage, or in an aluminum trash can with a lid near the compost pile.

ALTERNATE LAYERS AND STRIKE A HEALTHY CARBON-TO-NITROGEN RATIO. Create layers in your compost pile, starting with a 4-inch layer of twigs, hay, or straw to allow for good air circulation, followed by a layer of dried leaves and a layer of finished compost. If you're just starting out and don't have any homemade compost yet, you can purchase some at your local gardening store. Then alternate between layers of green (nitrogen-rich) material and brown (carbon-rich) material. Striking a healthy carbon-to-nitrogen ratio will speed up the process of decomposition. A good rule of thumb is to add four times as much carbon-rich ingredients as nitrogen-rich ingredients (by volume, not weight).

MAINTAIN YOUR COMPOST PILE OR BIN. While you could leave your compost to decompose on its own, a little maintenance goes a long way to speed up the process. For example, when you add fresh materials, be sure to mix them with the layers below it. Also, keep your compost the consistency of a wrung-out sponge—moist, but not too soggy. If it's too wet, add brown materials; if it's too dry, add green materials and/or water. Finally, using a shovel or pitchfork, mix or turn the compost once a week to introduce oxygen and eliminate odor.

USE YOUR FINISHED COMPOST. It can take anywhere from 2 weeks to 12 months to produce compost. You'll know it's ready when its dark and crumbly, with a pleasant, earthy smell. At that point, you can use it as a potting soil for houseplants, soil amendment for garden veggies and flowers, mulch around trees and shrubs, lawn top dressing, and compost "tea"—a rich, liquid fertilizer you can make by steeping compost in water.

MATERIALS THAT CAN BE COMPOSTED

Fruits and vegetables

Eggshells

Coffee grounds and filters

Tea bags

Nut shells

Shredded newspaper

Cardboard

Paper

Yard trimmings

Grass clippings

Houseplants

Hay and straw

Leaves

Sawdust

Wood chips

Wooden toothbrushes

Cotton and wool rags

Dryer and vacuum cleaner lint

Hair and fur

Fireplace ashes

MATERIALS THAT SHOULDN'T BE COMPOSTED

Black walnut tree leaves or twigs

Coal or charcoal ash

Meat and meat bones

Fish and fish bones

Dairy products

Eggs

Diseased or insect-ridden plants

Fats, grease, lard, or oils

Animal feces

Cat litter

Dead animals

Pressure-treated lumber

Sand

Yard trimmings treated with chemicals

Colored or glossy paper

DRYING HERBS

If you've ever grown herbs, you're probably accustomed to having more than you can possibly use in one season. Luckily, you can dry them and enjoy the bounty of summer all year long. If you harvest, dry, and store them properly, herbs can retain their flavor and medicinal value for up to a year. Here are a few tips:

HARVEST. It's important to harvest herbs at the right time. Pick after the flower buds appear but before they open, when the plant has the highest concentration of essential oils. It's also best to pick them in the morning, after the morning dew has evaporated but before the sun gets too hot.

CLEAN. Unless you plan to use them immediately, it's best to avoid washing herbs, as dampness promotes the growth of yeast and mold. Instead, remove old, dead, or wilted leaves by hand and clean by shaking or brushing away debris. Use organic gardening practices so you don't have to worry about washing off chemicals.

DRY. Air-drying works best for herbs with a low-moisture content, such as bay leaves, while freezing works best for herbs with a high-moisture content, such as basil. For low-moisture herbs, dry them in the dark with good air circulation and temperatures below 110°F. You can use a food dehydrator (set between 90° and 110°F), flat baskets, clean window screens, or clothes drying racks. Although it might seem like a good shortcut, microwaves and conventional ovens should be avoided, as they tend to cook and destroy the quality of herbs. You can also tie up herbs in bundles of 4 to 6 stems and hang them upside down to dry. To prevent contamination and oxidation, it's crucial to take down the bundles and store them as soon as they're dry—you'll know they've finished drying when you can crumble them easily in your hand.

STORE. Whole leaves and seeds retain oils better in storage than crumbled herbs or ground seeds. You can certainly use a mortar and pestle to grind your herbs, but bear in mind that they may not retain their quality as long. They tend to retain their flavor best if kept whole until you're ready to use them. Either way, store dried herbs in airtight containers out of direct sunlight and away from heat. Label jars immediately with the date and contents. You can tell if an herb is still valuable by its appearance, smell, and effectiveness. As the herbalist Rosemary Gladstar says, it should look, smell, and work just as it did on the day it finished drying. When using dried herbs in cooking, keep in mind that dried herbs are more concentrated than fresh. Generally speaking, if a recipe calls for 1 tablespoon fresh herbs, you should substitute 1 teaspoon crushed dried herbs.

FREEZING FRESH HERBS IN BUTTER OR OIL

One of my favorite ways to preserve herbs at the end of summer is to freeze them. Technically, you can freeze herbs on their own by placing them in an airtight container, but doing so often results in browning, freezer burn, and loss of flavor and aroma. A better way to preserve them is to freeze them in butter or olive oil in ice cube trays or silicone molds. Once frozen, the cubes can be used to add flavor to soups, stews, stir-fries, pastas, and marinades. The freeze-to-preserve method works best with hardier herbs like oregano, rosemary, sage, and thyme. Soft herbs like mint, basil, and dill don't do as well when frozen and are better used fresh.

TO FREEZE Carefully remove the herb leaves from the stems, discard any brown or wilted leaves, wash thoroughly, and pat dry. Chop or mince the leaves or keep them whole, depending on the type and intended use. Divide the herbs into ice cubes trays or silicone molds, filling each compartment about three-quarters of the way. Top off with melted butter or extra-virgin olive oil to fill each compartment. Freeze for at least 8 hours, then remove the cubes from the molds and transfer to a glass storage container or a silicone storage bag. Label the container with the type of herb and the date and store in the freezer for up to 3 months.

LOW-MOISTURE HERBS	HIGH-MOISTURE HERBS
Bay	Basil
Celery	Borage
Dill	Chives
Lemon balm	Cilantro
Lemon verbena	Lemongrass
Marjoram	Mint
Oregano	Parsley
Rosemary	
Sage	
Tarragon	
Thyme	

ORGANIC WEED CONTROL

I'm not against weeds. I understand that a weed is just a plant growing in the wrong place. That said, I can commiserate with the gardener who feels frustrated when weeds grow where she doesn't want them to grow—for example, in an in-ground bed where they compete with vegetables, in the cracks between bricks on the patio, or along gravel or mulch walkways.

This recipe makes a simple, nontoxic herbicide that you can whip up from ingredients in your cleaning supplies closet. The citrus contains an essential oil called D-limonene, which strips the cuticle right off the leaves of the weeds. Once stripped, the acetic acid in the vinegar dries out the foliage. The soap acts as a surfactant that helps reduce surface tension on the leaves, so that the plant can absorb the other ingredients and let them do their work. This herbicide is designed for light weeding—some hardier weeds won't seem fazed at all by household vinegar. It also doesn't work its way into the root system, so it may require multiple treatments. Still, it's a safe and practical solution for the light stuff, including weeds that pop up around walkways, fences, and patios.

INGREDIENTS

3 cups citrus all-purpose cleaner concentrate (page 74)

3 tablespoons citric acid

1½ teaspoons castile soap or Sal Suds

DIRECTIONS

In a 16-ounce spray bottle, combine the undiluted cleaner and citric acid. Screw on the spray cap and shake well to dissolve the citric acid. Add the soap and screw the cap on again. Tip the bottle upside down and right side up a few times to gently mix the ingredients.

TO USE Thoroughly spray the leaves and stems of weeds. Be sure to do it on a sunny day when you're not expecting rain, and be careful not to spray it on garden vegetables, as it won't discriminate between plants you want to keep and weeds you want to kill.

SAFETY TIP Keep cats away from treated areas for several hours after applying the herbicide, as the natural oils from the citrus peels are believed to be dangerous to them if ingested.

COMMON BENEFICIAL BUGS

Damsel bugs

Damselflies

Dragonflies

Fireflies

Ground beetles

Lacewings

Ladybugs

Parasitic wasps

Praying mantids

Predatory mites

Predatory stink bugs

Robber flies

Rove beetles

Soldier beetles

Spiders

ATTRACTING BENEFICIAL BUGS

Bugs get a bad rap. In the garden, we call them pests and curse them when they eat our vegetables. Sometimes we even go as far as to poison them with chemical pesticides. But according to researchers, 97 percent of all bugs are beneficial in some way—they either do no harm, provide food for other animals such as birds, or prey upon the insects that destroy our crops. Ironically enough, when we use chemical insecticides, we may end up eliminating the pests (for now), but we also eradicate the beneficial bugs that serve as natural pest control. Take the ladybug beetle as an example: A single adult ladybug will eat 50 aphids a day; her younglings will eat thousands of aphids, spider mites, and whiteflies in the same period of time.

Since beneficial bugs are so proficient at controlling pests, you'll want to attract them in droves to the garden. Here are a few tips:

CONSIDER THE GARDEN AN ACTIVE ECOSYSTEM. Instead of focusing on battling bad bugs with chemical pesticides, switch your focus to welcoming beneficial bugs, allowing the insect world to create a natural balance in your garden.

KNOW YOUR BUGS. Learn which bugs are beneficial and which ones are pests, as well as how to identify them.

PLANT THEIR FAVORITE FOODS. Plant a diverse mixture of plants that provide nectar and pollen to beneficial bugs, including plants in the daisy family (aster, cosmos, yarrow); plants in the carrot family (cilantro, dill, parsley, fennel); plants in the mustard family (alyssum); and buckwheats.

ADOPT THE PRINCIPLES OF COMPANION PLANTING. Employ this age-old strategy of placing plants together to attract beneficial insects and deter pests. For example, plant marigolds with tomatoes to deter nematodes, slugs, and tomato worms. Plant nasturtiums to draw aphids away from cucumbers, tomatoes, squash, and zucchini.

CREATE SHELTER OR HABITAT FOR BENEFICIAL BUGS. Beneficial bugs need places to feed, hide, reproduce, and overwinter. Create borders of diverse vegetation with flowers, shrubs, and grasses. Consider building an insect hotel (see page 226) and installing it in the fall when bugs are readying for winter and hibernation.

PROVIDE A WATER SOURCE. Provide a reliable source of clean water, using saucers, birdbaths, fountains, or water features. Change the water often to avoid attracting mosquitos.

LIMIT PESTICIDE USE. Choose nonchemical methods of insect control, including hand-picking pests, pruning away infestations, and using row covers.

INSECT HOTEL

If you're a gardener and a nature enthusiast, you'll love creating an insect hotel to welcome pollinators and other beneficial insects to your garden. With all of its nooks and crannies, it provides a vital haven for pollinating butterflies, solitary bees, lacewings, ladybugs, and other insects that help pollinate flowers, control pests, and maintain a healthy garden ecosystem. The best time to build and install an insect hotel is in the fall, when beneficial bugs start looking for a place to hibernate. Come spring, they'll be right there in your garden, ready to pollinate plants, decompose old plant matter, and devour unwanted pests.

An insect hotel is easy to make—you just need an open bird house or a wooden box with an overhang to protect it from rain and snow. Instructions for a simple box are below. Once you have your frame, fill it with various materials from nature to provide safe shelter and nesting fodder for your guests. You can use all manner of found, recycled, and upcycled materials, from twigs and wood chips to rolled-up paper, hollow plant stems, bamboo reeds, cardboard tubing, blocks of wood with holes, dried leaves, bark, straw, and hay. Generally speaking, solitary bees like to nest in hollow stems or holes drilled in blocks of wood; ladybugs like to hibernate between twigs or dried leaves packed together; beetles, centipedes, spiders, and woodlice love to hang out under rotting wood and bark.

MATERIALS

½-inch-by-4-inch rot-resistant wood board (you will need about 3 feet)

½-inch-by-5-inch rot-resistant wood board (you will need only 5½ inches but may need to buy a longer board)

1¼-inch weather-resistant screws

Wood glue

Twigs, wood chips, cut bamboo canes, blocks of wood with drilled holes, pinecones, dried leaves, bark, straw, and/or hay

Hanging hardware

continued

DIRECTIONS

1. For the sides of the box, cut two 9¼-inch pieces from the 4-inch-wide board. On each piece, mark one edge at 8¼ inches, draw a line from this mark to the top of the opposite corner, and cut on this line so that the top edge is angled.

2. For the back, cut a 9⅛-inch piece from the 4-inch-wide board.

3. For the middle and bottom pieces, cut two 4-inch lengths from the 4-inch-wide board.

4. For the roof, cut a 5½-inch piece from the 5-inch-wide board.

5. To assemble, place the side pieces on either side of the back piece (along the long edges) and screw through the outside of the side pieces into the long edges of the back board.

6. Insert the bottom piece and screw in both sides.

7. Glue the middle piece to the inside of the side pieces, and screw it in place, if you wish.

8. Attach the roof by lining it up with the back board so that it hangs over the front and sides. Screw through the roof into the side and back pieces.

9. Stack your filling materials in the box so they're packed tightly but still allow ample space for insects to enter and nest.

10. Attach hanging hardware to the box and fix it to a fence or tree trunk, about 3 feet off the ground, preferably facing south so your bugs can feel the warmth of the morning sun.

SAVING SEEDS

Saving seeds can be a cost-effective and rewarding way to garden. Not only does it save you money by eliminating the need to purchase seed packets and transplants year after year, but it also allows you to choose seeds from the strongest, best-performing plants. If you choose wisely, you can improve your seed stock, while conserving the genetic diversity of plants and the cultural heritage behind them. Below are a few guidelines.

PLANT HEIRLOOM OR OPEN-POLLINATED SEEDS. When planning your garden, plant with seed-saving in mind. Avoid hybrids and instead choose open-pollinated or heirloom plants that are likely to produce seeds that are "true to type," meaning they'll reproduce fruits or flowers with the same distinct characteristics as their parent plants. Not only do hybrids not breed true-to-type, but they also tend to be less genetically stable and vigorous as their parent seeds. Seeds will be marked OP, heirloom, or hybrid (F1) on their packages.

START WITH EASY, SELF-POLLINATING PLANTS. When getting started with seed-saving, it's best to start by planting easy, self-pollinating crops, such as tomatoes, peppers, beans, and peas. These crops are among the easiest to save because you don't need special botanical knowledge to ensure the seeds reproduce true-to-type. Plants that depend on wind or insects to pollinate, on the other hand, often produce hybrid seeds and make the process of saving seeds a bit trickier.

SAVE SEEDS FROM THE BEST PLANTS. When collecting seeds, put yourself in the mindset of a plant breeder. Gather from the healthiest, tastiest, and most robust plants. If you save seeds from the biggest, tastiest tomato in the garden and replant them the following year, you'll end up with seeds that produce similarly big, tasty tomatoes. Likewise, avoid weakling plants, including those that are disease-infested or flavorless.

HARVEST SEEDS WHEN MATURE AND ACCORDING TO PLANT TYPE. Wait until seeds are fully ripe before harvesting, as they won't germinate if picked too early. Also, learn how to harvest according to the type of plant.

- **FOR TOMATOES,** allow the fruit to ripen fully on the plant, then cut it open, scoop out the seeds, and place them, along with the gel surrounding them, in a bowl of water. Cover the bowl with cheesecloth and set it aside. The seeds will ferment and sink to the bottom within 3 to 5 days, at which time you can strain them, rinse them well, and spread them out to dry on newspaper for 1 to 2 weeks.

- **FOR PEPPERS,** allow a few fruits to stay on the plant until they mature and start to wrinkle. Then cut open the fruit, scoop out the seeds, and spread out on newspaper to dry for about a week.

- **FOR BEANS AND PEAS,** allow a few pods to stay on the plant until they are dry and starting to brown, with the seeds rattling inside. Strip the pods from the plant and allow them to dry intact on a plate or newspaper for 2 weeks. Once dry, remove the seeds for storage.

STORE SEEDS PROPERLY. Before storing, make sure seeds are completely dry to prevent mold or contamination. Once properly dried, seal seeds in paper envelopes or seed packets labeled with the name, variety, and date collected. To ensure longevity, place the seed packets in airtight glass jars and store in the refrigerator or another cool, dark place. If stored properly, most seeds can keep for several years.

BIRDSEED ORNAMENTS

When it comes to looking after our feathered friends, my children and I like to place lots of bird feeders in and around the garden, including just outside our kitchen window, where we can watch and enjoy them. We try to feed them year-round but make an extra effort during late winter and early spring, when their natural food sources are scarce or depleted. One of the many ways we feed the birds is by making these simple birdseed ornaments each year. Not only do they provide a rich sensory experience for young hands, but they also give the kids a way to connect with the natural world just outside their door.

MATERIALS

¼ cup unflavored powdered gelatin	*Cookie cutters*
½ cup cold water	*1 straw*
½ cup boiling water	*Biodegradable twine*
2½ cups birdseed	

DIRECTIONS

1. In a large bowl, mix the gelatin into the cold water until mostly dissolved. Add the boiling water and continue to mix until the gelatin is completely dissolved. Add the birdseed, about 1 cup at a time, and mix well so that the gelatin mixture coats each seed.

2. Line a rimmed baking sheet with compostable parchment paper and set the cookie cutters on it. Fill each cookie cutter about three-quarters of the way with birdseed mixture. Using your fingers or a small square of parchment paper, press the seed mixture firmly into the cutter. Add more seed mixture and keep pressing until it reaches the top edge of the cookie cutter. Make a hole for the twine by pushing the straw through the seed mixture and rotating it. Be sure to leave a thick edge between the hole and the top of the ornament.

3. Place the baking sheet in the refrigerator for a few hours, until the ornaments harden and gel. Once set, remove the ornaments from the cookie cutters by gently pushing at the edges until the ornament falls out. Thread twine through the holes and hang the ornaments on tree branches in your yard.

UPCYCLED TEACUP BIRD FEEDER

Another fun and inexpensive DIY bird feeder can be made from an old or second-hand teacup and saucer. If you can't find a matching set, don't fret—a mismatched pair adds charm and whimsy to the kitchen garden and, luckily, your birds won't care one bit. When you go looking for the perfect teacup, do try to find one with straight rather than V-shaped sides. Although you can make any teacup and saucer work, cups with straight sides (and straight handles) lend themselves to level bird feeders, once hung from a tree branch or shepherd's hook. Of course, with a little ingenuity and creativity, you can make any set work. It just might take a little more fine-tuning on your part.

MATERIALS

Teacup and saucer   *Shepherd's hook (optional)*

Strong glue   *Birdseed*

Twine

DIRECTIONS

Make sure the teacup and saucer are clean and dry. Place the teacup on its side with the handle sticking up, and locate the best place to glue it to the saucer. Once you've figured out where you want to glue it, lift the teacup where it meets the saucer and apply a small amount of glue to the saucer. Carefully, lower the teacup back into place and press it into the glue to secure it. Hold in place for a few minutes. If the glue is still wet, you can use painter's tape to hold the teacup down until it dries, which could take up to 2 hours depending on what kind of glue you use. Once the glue is dry, attach a piece of twine to the handle and hang it from a tree or shepherd's hook. Fill the teacup and saucer with birdseed and enjoy!

WILDFLOWER SEED BOMBS

Wildflower seed bombs are a great way to get children and nongardeners excited about growing plants. When it comes to making them, children love to participate—not only do they get to make a mess and get their hands dirty, but kids (and grown-ups, too!) often find mixing and molding clay to be relaxing and therapeutic. Made of clay, potting soil, and seeds, seed bombs are planted or thrown into an area, where they stay put because of the weight of the clay. Eventually they break down and sow themselves after a good rain. Wildflowers are pretty to look at, and they also create native habitats that support bees and butterflies. Some people like to plant them strategically in a garden box, planter, or garden bed. Others enjoy playing guerilla gardener, lobbing them into their own backyard, along rivers, in meadows, or in empty lots. Either way, after a few short weeks, they'll sprout into native wildflowers, making everything pop with color and beauty! I find that seed bombs make wonderful gifts for spring holidays, such as Earth Day, Spring Equinox, Easter, Passover, and Mother's Day. Simply wrap the finished bombs in fabric scraps or tissue paper and tie with twine, yarn, or string. Attach a name tag and give to friends and loved ones.

MATERIALS

1 part native wildflower seeds   *3 parts air-dry clay*

4 parts potting soil

DIRECTIONS

In a medium bowl, mix the seeds and soil. Add the clay and fold it into the seed-soil mixture. Slowly add warm water, just a little at a time, to soften the clay and make the mixture easier to combine. If it's too wet, add more soil; if it's too dry, add more water. Keep mixing with your hands until the mixture has the consistency of firm cookie dough. Grab small handfuls of the mixture and shape it into little bombs, the size of doughnut holes. Place the bombs on a rimmed baking sheet lined with compostable parchment paper and allow to dry and harden, which can take 1 to 2 days, depending on temperature and humidity.

REFRIGERATOR PICKLES

Kirby cucumbers are a staple in my kitchen garden, and pickles are my favorite way to prepare and eat them. There are many ways to pickle a cucumber, but brined and refrigerated is one of the easiest ways to make a fresh, crunchy pickle. If you've got 15 minutes, here's a great way to do it. **Makes 2 pints**

INGREDIENTS

1½ cups apple cider vinegar, store-bought or homemade (page 34)

1½ cups water

1 tablespoon pickling salt or kosher salt

1 pound Kirby cucumbers

4 garlic cloves

1 to 3 fresh dill sprigs

2 teaspoons dill seed

½ teaspoon mustard seeds

½ teaspoon black peppercorns

½ teaspoon crushed red pepper

DIRECTIONS

1. To prepare the pickling brine, combine the vinegar, water, and salt in a saucepan and heat over high heat, whisking, until the salt is dissolved. Transfer the brine to a clean quart-size jar and refrigerate until cool, about 30 minutes.

2. Wash 2 pint-size, wide-mouth canning jars. Wash and dry the cucumbers. Trim away the blossom ends and either leave the cucumbers whole or cut them into spears. Divide the garlic, dill sprigs and seeds, mustard seeds, peppercorns, and crushed red pepper between the jars. Pack the cucumbers into the jars. If they're too long, trim the ends until they fit. Pour the brine over the cucumbers until they're completely submerged. Tap the jars against the counter a few times to remove air bubbles. Screw the lids on the jars and refrigerate for 48 hours and then enjoy! The pickles will keep in the refrigerator for up to a month.

GRANDMA'S BASIC SAUERKRAUT

One of the great paradoxes of our time is that while 40 percent of all food produced is never eaten, one in eight Americans struggle to put food on the table. When I was growing up, I remember hearing about how my great-grandparents survived the Great Depression, not just because their families grew food but also because they knew how to put it by. One way they preserved food was by fermenting vegetables. I'm not sure if they knew then what we know now, but while boosting their food's shelf life, they were also creating healing foods rich in digestive enzymes and probiotic bacteria.

When my children were little and struggled with digestive issues, I picked up where my grandmother left off and learned everything I could about culturing gut-healing foods. I started with this sauerkraut recipe and then kept right on going to make yogurt, kimchi, kefir, kombucha, sourdough, and pickles. Although this recipe calls specifically for cabbage, I hope you'll use it as a gateway to fermenting other delicious vegetables. **Makes 1 quart**

INGREDIENTS

1 medium green cabbage   *1 to 3 tablespoons sea salt*

DIRECTIONS

Discard the wilted outer leaves of the cabbage. Cut the cabbage into quarters and trim out the core. Slice each quarter down its length, creating 8 wedges, then slice each wedge crosswise into very thin ribbons. Transfer the cabbage to a large mixing bowl. Add the salt and work it into the cabbage by massaging and squeezing the cabbage with your hands. Continue for about 10 minutes, until the cabbage becomes limp and starts to release its juices. Once the cabbage has released ample juices, begin packing it into a sterilized quart-size glass jar. Every so often, tamp down the cabbage so that the juices rise above it. Pour the leftover juices from your mixing bowl over the cabbage. When the jar is full, weight down the cabbage with a fermentation weight. If you don't have a fermentation weight, you can make one yourself using a cabbage core, an apple core, or a small jar (see box).

Seal the jar with a regular jar lid or an airlock lid. Airlock lids are designed to release pressure from the jar; if you don't have one, you'll just need to burp your ferment daily by unscrewing the jar lid to release the pressure and then screwing it back. Set the jar aside on your kitchen counter and allow the cabbage to ferment at room temperature for 2 to 3 weeks, depending on how sour you like it. Once the sauerkraut is ready, seal with an airtight lid and store it in the refrigerator for up to several months.

DIY FERMENTATION WEIGHT

CABBAGE CORE WEIGHT Cut a cabbage in half, remove the core, and trim it into the shape of a square or circle until it fits inside your jar. Notch a hole in the center to make it easier to remove from the jar with your finger.

APPLE CORE WEIGHT Peel and core an apple. Slice into 1-inch disks and trim the edges if necessary until they fit inside your jar. Place as many disks in the jar as needed to keep the vegetables submerged.

NESTED JAR WEIGHT Fill a smaller glass jar with water and nest it into the mouth of the fermentation jar.

FERMENTED RADISHES

Radishes are fun to plant, fun to grow, and fun to pick . . . but not that fun to eat. I can gobble down no more than three or four raw radishes before I start to wonder why I grew something I didn't actually want to eat. But when lacto-fermented, the bitter, earthy veggie turns into a crunchy, sour treat. It's also one of the easiest and most beautiful vegetables to culture. The color leaches out of the skin and into the brine and dyes everything fuchsia. **Makes 2 pints**

INGREDIENTS

$2^1/_2$ tablespoons salt

4 cups filtered water

2 to 3 bunches radishes

6 fresh dill sprigs

4 whole garlic cloves

$^1/_2$ teaspoon mustard seeds

$^1/_2$ teaspoon black peppercorns

DIRECTIONS

Prepare the brine by dissolving the salt in the filtered water in a bowl or large measuring cup with a spout. Wash the radishes. Trim away the stems and cut the radishes into quarters (you will need about 2½ cups). Divide the dill, garlic, mustard seeds, and peppercorns between 2 clean pint-size wide-mouth canning jars. Pack the radishes into the jars. Pour the brine over the radishes and place a fermentation weight on top of the radishes to keep them fully submerged and protected from bacteria. If you don't have a fermentation weight, you can make one yourself (see page 241). Seal your jars with a regular jar lid or an airlock lid. Airlock lids are designed to release pressure; if you don't have one, you'll just need to burp your ferment daily by unscrewing the jar lid to release the pressure and then screwing it back. Set aside on your kitchen counter and allow to ferment at room temperature for 3 to 7 days, depending on how sour you want them. Remove the fermentation weight, seal the jar with an airtight lid, and store in the refrigerator for up to 3 months.

FERMENTED SALSA

By midsummer, I'm usually racking my brain for ways to preserve my small bounty of tomatoes. Thankfully, tomatoes and preservation go together like peanut butter and jelly. Tomatoes lend themselves well to canning, drying, freezing, and fermenting, which makes them an ideal candidate for stocking your larder for the winter. I love rolling up my sleeves and having a little canning party, but I also love to ferment fruits and vegetables. Whereas homemade salsa lasts only a few days in the refrigerator, fermented salsa lasts for months. And since it's cultured, it's a wonderful way to add more probiotic foods to your diet. **Makes about 1 quart**

INGREDIENTS

3 medium tomatoes, diced

1 medium onion, diced

1 medium green bell pepper, seeded and diced

1 or 2 jalapeños, seeded and diced

2 or 3 scallions, green parts only, minced

2 garlic cloves, minced

¼ cup fresh cilantro, minced

Fresh lemon juice, to taste

2 teaspoons salt

DIRECTIONS

Combine all the ingredients in a clean quart-size canning jar. Press the ingredients down to release the liquids from the vegetables. Continue to press until all the vegetables are submerged under the liquid. Place a fermentation weight on top of the vegetables to weight them down and keep them submerged and protected from bacteria. If you don't have a fermentation weight, you can make one yourself (see page 241). Seal the jar with a regular jar lid or an airlock lid. Airlock lids are designed to release pressure from the jar; if you don't have one, you'll just need to burp your ferment daily by unscrewing the jar lid to release the pressure and then screwing it back. Set aside on your kitchen counter and allow to ferment at room temperature for 2 days. Remove the fermentation weight, seal the jar with an airtight lid, and store in the refrigerator for up to 3 months.

TOMATO-CARROT SOUP

A great way to use up all your mid- to late-summer tomatoes is to make soup. You can enjoy it immediately or freeze it for a mid-winter taste of summer. A few years ago, when I noticed my tomatoes and carrots were ripening at the same time, I made this hearty tomato-carrot soup. It's since become a family favorite. Served with homemade artisan bread (see page 38), it makes the perfect comfort food throughout the year. **Makes 2 quarts**

INGREDIENTS

4 pounds tomatoes, peeled and halved

¾ cup olive oil, ghee, or butter

1 teaspoon salt

½ teaspoon ground black pepper

1 medium yellow onion, chopped

4 garlic cloves, chopped

2 celery ribs, diced

5 medium carrots, diced

2 cups chicken or veggie stock, store-bought or homemade (page 32)

¾ cup coconut milk or heavy cream

½ cup chopped fresh basil leaves

DIRECTIONS

1. Preheat the oven to 400°F.

2. Place the tomato halves on a rimmed baking sheet. Reserve 3 tablespoons of the oil, then drizzle the rest over the tomatoes. Sprinkle with the salt and pepper. Roast for 30 to 40 minutes, until the tomatoes are golden brown.

3. Meanwhile, heat the reserved 3 tablespoons oil in a large pot over medium heat. Add the onion, garlic, celery, and carrots and cook until the vegetables are softened. When the tomatoes have finished roasting, add them to the pot with the vegetables. Add the stock, reduce the heat to low, and simmer for 10 to 15 minutes, until the vegetables are tender. Using an immersion or countertop blender, puree the soup. Serve immediately, drizzling each serving with coconut milk and garnishing with basil. To store leftovers (without the coconut milk or basil), allow to cool, then transfer to airtight containers and freeze for up to 6 months.

Top left: Tomato-Carrot Soup (above); top right: Waste-Free Broccoli Stalk Soup (page 250); bottom left: Roasted Garlic Soup (page 251); bottom right: Chilled Cucumber-Avocado Soup (page 249)

CARROT TOP PESTO

If there's one thing I love more than basil pesto, it's pesto made from food scraps that would normally be cast aside and tossed into the compost bucket. In this case, I'm referring to carrot tops, those spindly greens that seem to serve no other purpose than to help gardeners heave the orange roots from the soil. As it turns out, those leaves can be used to make a pesto that is every bit as delicious as the traditional one made from basil. And just like basil pesto, it goes well with bread, crackers, pasta, and raw veggies. **Makes about 1 cup**

INGREDIENTS

1 cup carrot greens

¼ cup pistachios

2 garlic cloves, peeled

2 tablespoons fresh lemon juice

3 tablespoons extra-virgin olive oil

½ avocado, peeled (optional)

Salt and ground black pepper

DIRECTIONS

Combine the carrot greens, pistachios, garlic, and lemon juice in a blender or food processor. Blend until a chunky paste forms. You may need to stop occasionally to scrape down the sides. Add the olive oil, 1 tablespoon at a time, until combined. If you want to make the pesto creamier, add the avocado and blend until a creamy paste forms. Season with salt and pepper to taste. Serve immediately or store in airtight containers in the refrigerator for up to 4 days.

CHILLED CUCUMBER-AVOCADO SOUP

This summer soup is the perfect way to get your soup fix on a hot summer day, all while using up fresh cucumbers and herbs from the garden. What's more, it's a cold soup, which means you won't even have to turn on the stove to prepare it. The cucumber and mint are cooling and refreshing, and you can enjoy it with or without yogurt, depending on whether you're in the mood for a lighter or heavier meal. To make it vegan, feel free to use a nondairy yogurt—otherwise, Greek yogurt works especially well. **Makes about 1½ quarts if using the yogurt or 1 quart without**

INGREDIENTS

2 English cucumbers, chopped

2 ripe avocados, peeled and pitted, plus more for garnish

2 cups plain yogurt (optional)

1 cup water

¼ cup fresh lemon juice

1 tablespoon olive oil

⅔ cup packed whole fresh mint leaves

¼ cup chopped fresh flat-leaf parsley

¼ cup chopped fresh chives, plus more for garnish

Sea salt, to taste

DIRECTIONS

Combine all the ingredients except the salt in a blender and blend until smooth. Season with salt to taste. Transfer to airtight jars and refrigerate until fully chilled, 1 to 2 hours. Enjoy cold, garnished with diced avocado and chopped chives.

WASTE-FREE BROCCOLI STALK SOUP

Broccoli stalks might be one of the most underappreciated vegetables on the planet. Even grocery stores are giving up on them, selling broccoli crowns without stalks or florets by the bag. Here's the thing: Those stalks actually keep the florets from going bad and—get this—they taste really good, too! They're also nutritious—just like the florets, broccoli stalks are packed with vitamin C, potassium, B vitamins, calcium, and iron. One way I like to use them is with their florets in this warm and hearty fall soup. Serve with no-knead artisan bread (page 38). **Makes about 4 quarts**

INGREDIENTS

2 tablespoons unrefined coconut oil

1 medium onion, chopped

1 celery rib, chopped

1 leek, trimmed and sliced

3 garlic cloves, chopped

1 teaspoon chopped fresh flat-leaf parsley

1½ pounds broccoli florets and stalks, ends removed, tough woody layers peeled, and chopped (about 8 cups)

2 medium Yukon potatoes, chopped

8 cups vegetable stock, store-bought or homemade (page 32)

4 cups fresh spinach, stems removed

One 14-ounce can full-fat coconut milk

1 to 2 tablespoons fresh lemon juice, to taste

Kosher salt and ground black pepper, to taste

DIRECTIONS

In a large pot, melt the coconut oil over medium heat. Add the onion, celery, and leek and sauté until tender and translucent, 10 to 15 minutes. Add the garlic and parsley and cook until fragrant, about 30 seconds. Add the broccoli, potato, and stock. Bring to a boil over high heat, then reduce to a simmer. Cook until the vegetables are tender, about 20 minutes. Add the spinach and cook for 1 minute. Remove the pot from the heat and puree the soup using an immersion blender. (Alternatively, you can transfer the soup, in batches if necessary, to a countertop blender. When blending hot liquids, be sure to remove the center cap from the lid and hold a clean dish towel over the hole to allow steam to escape.) Transfer the pureed soup back to the pot. Stir in the coconut milk and heat for about a minute. Remove from the heat and add the lemon juice, salt, and pepper. Serve warm. To store leftovers, allow the soup to cool, then transfer it to airtight containers. Freeze for up to 6 months.

ROASTED GARLIC SOUP

This recipe could just as easily go in the natural wellness section. With four whole heads of garlic as its main ingredient, it's sure to boost the immune system and help you gear up for cold and flu season. I like to plant an entire bed of garlic in the fall so that come late summer, I have enough to meet all of my autumnal culinary and medicinal needs. If you're concerned that the flavor will be too overpowering, don't worry—roasting softens the garlic's sharpness and leads the way to a creamy, hearty soup. **Makes about 2 quarts**

INGREDIENTS

4 heads garlic, cloves separated and peeled

2 medium yellow onions, chopped

1 head cauliflower, chopped

2 tablespoons coconut oil

1 teaspoon salt

1 cup vegetable stock, store-bought or homemade (page 32)

2 cups coconut milk

1½ teaspoons fresh lemon juice

1 teaspoon chopped fresh thyme

Olive oil, for serving

DIRECTIONS

1. Preheat the oven to 400°F. Lined a rimmed baking sheet with compostable parchment paper.

2. Combine the garlic, onions, and cauliflower in a large bowl and toss with the coconut oil. Transfer the vegetables to the prepared baking sheet, spread out in a single layer, and sprinkle with the salt. Roast for 30 minutes.

3. Transfer the roasted vegetables to a large pot. Add the stock and coconut milk and cook over medium heat just until warmed, then blend with an immersion blender until creamy. (Alternatively, you can transfer the soup, in batches if necessary, to a countertop blender. When blending hot liquids, be sure to remove the center cap from the lid and hold a clean dish towel over the hole to allow steam to escape. Transfer the pureed soup back to the pot.) Taste and adjust seasonings. Serve garnished with the lemon juice, thyme, and a drizzle of olive oil.

TRADITIONAL BEET KVASS

When Hippocrates said "Let food be thy medicine," he may have been talking about beet kvass. Well, not likely—but he might as well have been. Beet kvass, a fermented beet drink, has been used as a tonic in Eastern Europe since the Middle Ages, when it was known to offer protection against infection. When I prepare and drink beet kvass, it's for its medicinal rather than epicurean qualities, which is to say it doesn't taste great, but I drink it anyway! According to Sally Fallon, author of *Nourishing Traditions,* beet kvass promotes regularity, aids digestion, cleanses the liver, and helps treat kidney stones. Like all fermented foods, it's also a way to put food by if you've got a bounty and don't want anything to go to waste. **Makes 3 cups**

INGREDIENTS

1 large beet, peeled and cut into 1½-inch pieces

1 tablespoon peeled and chopped fresh ginger

1 teaspoon sea salt

3 cups filtered water

DIRECTIONS

Wash and dry a quart-size canning jar and lid. Put the beets and ginger in the jar. Add the salt and water, leaving 1 inch of headspace at the top of the jar. Cover the jar with an airlock lid or a regular lid. If using a regular lid, be sure to burp the jar daily by opening the lid to release excess pressure. Allow the kvass to ferment at room temperature for 5 to 7 days. After 5 days, taste the kvass. It should have an earthy, tangy flavor. If not, screw the lid back on and give it 1 to 2 more days to ferment on the counter. When ready, strain out the solids and either eat them in a salad or compost them. Pour the reserved liquid into a clean quart-size jar with a tight-fitting lid and store in the refrigerator for up to 3 months.

NOTE If you don't enjoy beet kvass straight, you can reap the benefits by diluting it with sparkling water, adding it to soups, or using it as a substitute for vinegar in homemade salad dressings.

SAUTÉED BEET GREENS WITH PINE NUTS

After you've used your beets to make the kvass on page 252 (or prepared them another way), you'll be left with the greens. They are perfectly edible and, like other dark leafy greens, nutritious, too. To minimize food waste, chop them up and add them to soups, stews, or a sauté like this one. **Serves 2**

INGREDIENTS

¼ cup pine nuts

1 pound beet greens
(from 2 large or 3 small bunches)

1 tablespoon coconut oil

1 cup chopped sweet onion

¼ cup balsamic vinegar

2 garlic cloves, minced

½ cup water

Salt and ground black pepper

DIRECTIONS

1. Place a large skillet over medium heat. Add the pine nuts to the pan and toast until they are fragrant and golden brown. Stir and toss them frequently to prevent them from burning. Remove them from the pan and set aside.

2. Rinse and drain the beet greens. Remove the tough stems and chop the leaves into bite-size pieces.

3. In the same skillet, heat the coconut oil over medium heat. Add the onion and sauté for about a minute. Reduce the heat to low and continue to cook the onion for about 20 minutes, stirring occasionally, until soft and golden. Add the balsamic vinegar. Cook for 20 to 25 minutes to reduce the vinegar. Raise the heat to medium, add the garlic, and cook for about 2 minutes more. Add the water, bring to a boil, then add the greens. Toss everything together, reduce the heat to low, cover, and cook for 5 to 10 minutes, until the leaves are soft but still green. Remove from the heat, season with salt and pepper to taste, and toss with the pine nuts. Serve immediately.

HERBAL SALT

By summer's end, I usually have so many herbs, I don't know what to do with them all. They're often hanging from every peg or hook I can find in the house, waiting to be turned into teas, salves, spices, and—in this case—herbal sea salt. It makes a lovely homemade gift and can be added to just about any savory culinary dish from stews and roasts to eggs, veggies, grains, pasta, beans, and even popcorn! **Makes about ¾ cup**

INGREDIENTS

5 garlic cloves, peeled

½ cup kosher salt

2 cups fresh herbs (such as flat-leaf parsley, sage, rosemary, thyme, basil, cilantro, or mint)

DIRECTIONS

Put the garlic in a food processor, add 2 tablespoons of the sea salt, and pulse until finely ground. Add the herbs. Pulse until the mixture is like coarse sand. Be careful not to mix so long that it becomes a paste. Transfer the mixture to a rimmed baking sheet, sprinkle with the remaining 6 tablespoons sea salt, and mix well. Spread the herbal salt out on the baking sheet and leave it near an open window for a couple of days to dry. (Alternatively, use a food dehydrator set on 90° to 110°F.) Store the herbal salt in a clean, dry glass jar with a tight-fitted lid for up to 6 months.

HERBAL SIMPLE SYRUP

A great way to enjoy seasonal herbs and preserve them throughout the year is by using them to make simple syrups. If you've ever made or ordered a cocktail, you're probably familiar with simple syrup—it's essentially liquefied sugar made from two "simple" ingredients: water and sugar. I like to take it a step further by infusing it with herbs, my favorites being mint and thyme, although basil, lavender, lemon balm, lemon verbena, and rosemary make lovely syrups, too! If you're not a drinker, you can use simple syrup to create alcohol-free beverages. Just add a splash to water, tea, soda, or juice. You can also use it to sweeten fruit salads, yogurt, waffles, or pancakes or to dress up ice cream, cake, and other baked goods. This recipe is made the traditional way, prepared with 1 part water to 1 part sugar, but you can double the amount of sugar if you prefer a thicker, sweeter syrup. **Makes 1½ cups**

INGREDIENTS

1 cup water

1 cup sugar

8 fresh herb sprigs or a handful of fresh herb leaves

DIRECTIONS

Combine the water and sugar in a saucepan and simmer over medium heat, stirring constantly. When the sugar has dissolved, remove the saucepan from the heat and add the herbs. Cover with a lid and allow to steep for 30 minutes. Use a slotted spoon to remove the herbs from the syrup. Pour the syrup through a fine-mesh strainer into glass bottles or jars. Seal with airtight lids and store in the refrigerator for up to 2 weeks.

VINEGAR OF FOUR THIEVES

According to legend, as the bubonic plague raged through Europe, the town of Marseille was beset with four thieves who plundered the homes of the sick and dead without ever falling ill. When they were eventually caught, a judge agreed to pardon them if they would reveal their secret to maintaining good health. Their secret? An infusion of four herbs: sage, lavender, rosemary, and thyme. What I love about this vinegar is it's versatility. Not only is it useful as a tonic, but it can also serve as an insect repellent, an immune booster, a disinfectant spray, and a salad dressing. **Makes 1 quart**

INGREDIENTS

2 tablespoons dried sage

2 tablespoons dried lavender

2 tablespoons dried rosemary

2 tablespoons dried thyme

¼ teaspoon black peppercorns

4 to 8 garlic cloves, peeled

1 teaspoon grated lemon zest

4 cups raw apple cider vinegar, store-bought or homemade (page 34)

DIRECTIONS

Combine the herbs, peppercorns, garlic, and lemon zest in a quart-size glass jar and pour in the vinegar. Cover with the lid; if using a metal lid, place a piece of parchment paper between the jar and lid to prevent corrosion. Leave in a cool, dry place and allow to infuse for 4 to 6 weeks—the longer you leave it, the more flavorful or potent it will be. Strain the vinegar and compost the scraps.

TO USE

VINAIGRETTE Use in place of the lemon juice or vinegar when making simple vinaigrette (page 57).

INSECT REPELLENT Pour ¼ cup into an 8-ounce spray bottle. Fill the rest with water.

IMMUNE BOOSTER When you feel a cold or flu coming on, take 1 to 2 tablespoons every 3 to 4 hours until you feel better. As a preventative, take 1 tablespoon a day.

DISINFECTANT CLEANING SPRAY Combine with an equal amount of water in a spray bottle and use as an all-purpose disinfectant cleaner.

OLD-FASHIONED STRAWBERRY JAM

I can't imagine a sweeter way to preserve summer than by making strawberry jam. And even better—making it the old-fashioned way with three simple ingredients. Blackberries and raspberries work well, too. **Makes 4 pints**

INGREDIENTS

8 cups hulled strawberries   *2 tablespoons fresh lemon juice*

6 cups sugar

DIRECTIONS

1. Quarter the strawberries and combine them in a bowl with the sugar. Gently stir the strawberries until they're well coated with the sugar. Cover the bowl with a tea towel and leave it at room temperature for 2 hours.

2. Transfer the strawberries and sugar to a large stockpot and cook over low heat, stirring gently, until the sugar dissolves. Bring the mixture to a simmer, then transfer it to a glass or ceramic bowl, cover with a tea towel, and refrigerate overnight.

3. Before you proceed to the next step, sterilize 8 half-pint canning jars. To do so, remove the lids and set the glass jars in a stockpot full of water so that they are submerged. Bring the water to a boil and boil the jars for 10 minutes. Remove from the heat and allow to cool.

4. Transfer the chilled strawberry-sugar mixture to a clean stockpot and add the lemon juice. Bring the mixture to a boil over medium-high heat. Boil, stirring constantly and skimming off any foam that forms on the top, for 10 to 15 minutes, until the berries begin to thicken and gel. Reduce the heat to low and continue to cook for 5 minutes. The jam should set at around 220°F. (If you do not have a candy thermometer, place a plate in the freezer for 1 hour beforehand. When you think the jam has set, scoop a small dollop of jam onto the cold plate and run your finger through the middle of it. If it stays divided and doesn't run back together, it's set; if not, continue cooking the jam until you're sure it's set.)

5. Once it's ready, transfer the jam to the sterilized jars, leaving ¼ to ½ inch headspace, and seal. If you are planning to eat the jam over the next couple of months, refrigerate it. Otherwise, preserve it by processing it in a water bath: Set a canning rack in a large stockpot. Set the sealed jars of jam on the rack. Pour water into the pot so that the water level is 1 to 2 inches above the jars. Bring the water to a boil, cover the pot, and boil for 10 minutes. Remove the pot from the heat and allow the jars to cool in the pot for 5 minutes. Using canning tongs, remove the jars from the pot and set on a towel on the counter until completely cool, usually about 12 hours. Store the unopened jars in a cool, dark place for up to 18 months; refrigerate after opening.

RESOURCES

BOOKS

ZERO-WASTE

Cradle to Cradle: Remaking the Way We Make Things by Michael Braungart and William McDonough

Waste-Free Kitchen Handbook: A Guide to Eating Well and Saving Money by Wasting Less Food by Dana Gunders

Zero Waste Home: The Ultimate Guide to Simplifying Your Home by Reducing Your Waste by Bea Johnson

FOOD PRESERVATION

Wild Fermentation: The Flavor, Nutrition, and Craft of Live-Culture Foods by Sandor Ellix Katz

Ball Complete Book of Home Preserving: 400 Delicious and Creative Recipes for Today by Judi Kingry and Lauren Devine

Traditionally Fermented Foods: Innovative Recipes and Old-Fashioned Techniques for Sustainable Eating by Shannon Stonger

Nourishing Traditions: A Cookbook that Challenges Politically Correct Nutrition and the Diet Dictocrats by Sally Fallon

SIMPLE LIVING

Simple Matters: Living with Less and Ending Up with More by Erin Boyle

The Simple Home: A Month-by-Month Guide to Self-Reliance, Productivity and Contentment by Rhonda Hetzel

NATURAL CLEANING

Clean Mama's Guide to a Healthy Home: The Simple, Room-by-Room Plan for a Natural Home by Becky Rapinchuk

Natural Household Cleaning: Making Your Own Eco-Savvy Cleaning Products by Rachelle Strauss

HERBALISM

Healing Herbal Infusions: Simple and Effective Home Remedies for Colds, Muscle Pain, Upset Stomach, Stress, Skin Issues, and More by Colleen Codekas

Alchemy of Herbs: Transform Everyday Ingredients into Foods and Remedies That Heal by Rosalee De La Forêt

A Modern Herbal: Plant-Based Medicine for a Calmer, Healthier Life by Alys Fowler

Herbal Remedies for Vibrant Health: 175 Teas, Tonics, Oils, Salves, Tinctures, and Other Natural Remedies for the Entire Family by Rosemary Gladstar

Medicinal Herbs: A Beginner's Guide: 33 Herbs to Know, Grow, and Use by Rosemary Gladstar

The New American Herbal by Stephen Orr

NATURAL BATH AND BODY

200 Tips, Techniques, and Recipes for Natural Beauty by Shannon Buck

Herbs for Natural Beauty: Create Your Own Herbal Shampoos, Cleansers, Creams, Bath Blends, and More by Rosemary Gladstar

GARDENING

Small-Space Vegetable Gardens: Growing Great Edibles in Containers, Raised Beds, and Small Plots by Andrea Bellamy

The Bee-Friendly Garden: Design an Abundant Flower-Filled Garden That Nurtures Bees and Supports Biodiversity by Kate Frey and Gretchen LeBuhn

The Backyard Homestead: Produce All the Food You Need on Just a Quarter Acre by Carleen Madigan

Attracting Beneficial Bugs to Your Garden: A Natural Approach to Pest Control by Jessica Walliser

WEBSITES

Environmental Protection Agency: www.epa.gov

Environmental Working Group: www.ewg.org

Litterless blog (for a zero-waste grocery guide by state): www.litterless.com

Our World in Data: www.ourworldindata.org

Skin Deep Cosmetics Database: www.ewg.org/skindeep

United Nations Environment Programme: www.unenvironment.org

Zero Waste Collective: www.thezerowastecollective.com

ONLINE HERBAL STUDIES AND COURSES

Chestnut School of Herbal Medicine: www.chestnutherbs.com

Herbal Academy: www.theherbalacademy.com

SUPPLIES

BULK HERBS, ESSENTIAL OILS, BEESWAX, BUTTERS, CARRIER OILS, SMALL JARS, TINS, AND TUBES

Mountain Rose Herbs: www.mountainroseherbs.com

FERMENTATION SUPPLIES

Cultures for Health: www.culturesforhealth.com

GLASS JARS

Ball Canning Jars: www.ball.com

Fillmore Container: www.fillmorecontainer.com

Weck Jars: www.weckjars.com

INSECT HOTELS

Wudwerx shop: www.etsy.com

REUSABLE BEESWAX FOOD WRAPS

Abeego: www.abeego.com

REUSABLE CLOTH SHOPPING AND BULK BAGS

Dans le Sac: www.danslesac.co

EcoBags: www.ecobags.com

REUSABLE SILICONE STORAGE BAGS

Stasher Bag: www.stasherbag.com

ZERO-WASTE SUPPLIES FOR THE HOME (NATURAL CLEANING TOOLS, REUSABLE CONTAINERS, CLOTH LINEN, ETC.,)

June Home Supply: www.junehomesupply.com

Wild Minimalist: www.wildminimalist.com

ACKNOWLEDGMENTS

A big thank you to the readers and followers of Simply Living Well. Without your interest and encouragement, there would be no book, let alone anyone to read it! To the zero-waste community, for being such a kind and supportive group—I've learned a lot from you and am continually inspired by your dedication and wisdom.

To my husband, Scott, for supporting and believing in me; testing recipes and remedies; solo parenting our children while I wrote and photographed this book; helping me lug home secondhand furniture; using all of the reusable mugs, cups, and totes I stuff into your pockets and bags; helping me create the ideal kitchen garden; and agreeing to reconfigure your career and move cross-country twice, simply because it felt like the right thing to do.

To my children, Benjamin and Eloise, for being the best teachers; giving me a reason to care more than I already did; sampling countless recipes and remedies; giving honest feedback; lending a hand in the garden; and above all else, putting up with a mother who brings reusable silverware and canvas tote bags wherever we go. This book is dedicated to you and your great-grandparents—because they lit up for me the way I hope I light up for you.

To my literary agent, Julia Eagleton, for finding me, proposing the idea of writing a book, and helping find potential publishers for it. To your team at The Gernert Company for identifying international publishers to translate the book into multiple languages. To my editor, Stephanie Fletcher, and everyone at Houghton Mifflin Harcourt for believing in this project and using the most collaborative process an author could hope for. To Stephanie (again), copy editor Karen Wise, and production editor Rebecca Springer for your meticulous editing and attention to detail. To designer Ashley Lima and art director Melissa Lotfy for turning my words and photos into these beautiful pages, and to Breanne Sommer, Brooke Borneman, and Brianna Yamashita, for taking the reins on marketing and publicity.

To Melissa Egan—it was so fun working on a proposal with you! Thank you for listening well, helping me put my ideas on to paper, and introducing me to Chelsea Coolsaet, who helped design the most beautiful website for my blog and this book.

To my parents, for your unconditional love and the liberty to do my own thing, be my own person, and live a little out of the box. To my parents-in-law, for your unwavering support and devotion to our family, including the many hours you spent playing with Benjamin and Eloise, and feeding them the best home-cooked meals. And last, but certainly not least, to my grandparents (Mimi and Papa) for modeling what it means to live simply, slowly, and well.

INDEX